# CARO'S BOOK OF
# POKER
# TELLS

# CARO'S BOOK OF
# POKER
# TELLS

## THE PSYCHOLOGY AND
## BODY LANGUAGE OF POKER

## Mike Caro

THIS CARDOZA EDITION
IS PRINTED BY SPECIAL
ARRANGEMENT WITH
MIKE CARO UNIVERSITY
OF POKER PRESS.

MIKE ♠ CARO

*The Advanced School of Winning!*
POKER · GAMING · LIFE STRATEGY

# CARDOZA PUBLISHING

Mike Caro University is housed in Hollywood Park-Casino, Mike Caro University of Poker Gaming and Life Strategy (MCU) merges Caro's own research with the collective wisdom of other great poker minds to form a one-of-a-kind learning center teaching poker strategy and psychology. In addition to instructional courses, MCU serves as a central force for popularizing poker, maintaining its integrity, and standardizing rules. Contact MCU's website at: UniversityofPoker.com. To join the mailing list: Join@caro.com. To contact the author: caro@caro.com.

Cardoza Publishing is the foremost gaming and gambling publisher in the world with a library of almost 100 up-to-date and easy-to-read books and strategies. These authoritative works are written by the top experts in their fields and with more than 6,500,000 books in print, represent the best-selling and most popular gaming books anywhere.

Copyright © 2003 by Mike Caro
- All Rights Reserved -

Library of Congress Catalog No: 2002106098
ISBN: 1-58042-082-6

**This Cardoza edition is printed by special arrangement with Mike Caro University of Poker Press.** You may use up to 250 words in any copyrighted review, book, commentary or article if you attribute the quoted material to *Caro's Book of Poker Tells*, and its author, Mike Caro.

Visit our new web site (www.cardozapub.com) or write us for a full list of books, advanced and computer strategies.

### CARDOZA PUBLISHING
PO Box 1500 Cooper Station, New York, NY 10276
Phone (800)577-WINS
email: cardozapub@aol.com
### www.cardozapub.com

# TABLE OF CONTENTS

# ABOUT THE AUTHOR

For many years Mike Caro, legendary as "the Mad Genius of Poker," has clarified and pioneered some of the most important gambling concepts ever put on paper. He is consultant to many of the world's leading poker players and casinos, and his advice on casino games and gambling in general is highly regarded throughout the world.

Caro is primarily known as a teacher and theorist, but beyond that—twice world poker champion Doyle Brunson calls him "the best draw poker player alive," while the late gambling expert John Scarne ranked him in the top five, and premier authority David Sklansky has also rated him first in the world in that important category. But today, draw poker isn't even Mike Caro's strongest game. Most of his recent breakthrough research has been in hold 'em, seven-card stud, and other popular forms of poker.

## RESEARCH AND MORE

His in-depth statistics on poker and gambling are among the most widely quoted today. Caro is a computer wizard who uses his exclusive programs to back up his research. In addition, he is famous for his work on the psychology and philosophy of gambling. His personally programmed, artificially intelligent poker player—Orac (Caro spelled backwards)—astonished the scientific, gambling, and poker communities when it was able to play world-class, heads-up, no-limit hold 'em blow-for-blow against the best human players alive in 1984. This nationally televised, widely publicized feat hasn't been duplicated to this day.

Caro's standing-room-only seminars often draw upwards of 400 serious players from throughout the world. He is the founder of Mike Caro University of Poker, Gaming, and Life Strategy, and his expertise and accomplishments have been cited in publications from *Newsweek* to *Playboy* and in over fifty books other than his own.

Caro is known as "The Mad Genius" for good reason. Much of his teaching is unconventional and very profound. Yet he explains things in crisp, clear language that will have your pulse racing as you learn the secret keys to winning.

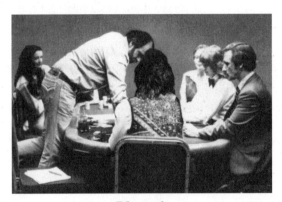

***Photo 1:***
*"Mad Genius" Mike Caro leans on the poker table during one of six tells photo sessions circa 1983. In all, more than 100 players, managers, experts and casino employees contributed to the making of the original Mike Caro's Book of Tells. This photo session was held at the Bingo Palace (now known as the Palace Station) in Las Vegas. Poker room manager Steve Schlemmer is at the right.*

***Photo 2:***
*Here, Caro addresses the largest paid audience that ever gathered for a one-man poker seminar until that night. The subject of his lecture, given at the Palace Station in Las Vegas, was "All Tells, Only Tells." While such attendance (158) seems paltry by Caro's standards today, the landmark seminar marked a growing interest in the science of poker. Caro has been at the forefront of this resurgence for almost twenty-five years running.*

# INTRODUCTION

Once you've mastered the basic elements of a winning poker formula, psychology becomes the key ingredient in separating break-even players from players who win consistently. The most profitable kind of poker psychology is the ability to read your opponents. Imagine the edge having this ability would give you and then imagine how much money you could win with it! This is exactly what I'll show you in this book. Bring this knowledge to the poker table and you will win money—it's as simple as that!

Any mannerism which helps you determine the secrets of an opponent's hand is called a *tell*. Look closely and you'll see opponents giving away the strength of their hands just by their mannerisms. Until a few years ago, nobody understood tells thoroughly. Experienced players would try to uncover trends in their opponents' behavior. Maybe they discovered that one opponent would always loosen his tie five minutes before attempting a major bluff. Such discoveries are important, but there's a much better way to go about reading opponents—and that's what you'll learn in this book.

If you wanted to catalog all the possible tells an opponent might exhibit, the list might go on forever. You could sit for a few days and jot down several thousand things that opponents might do under stress.

Unfortunately, after all that work, your list would be

pitifully incomplete. There are millions of tells you could write down if you could only think of them all.

There is a simple way to read your opponents. You must learn the motives behind their actions. Then, even when you encounter a tell you've never seen before, you'll have a good idea of what it means. When you're finished with this book, you won't have to memorize all the actions of each opponent. Instead, you'll be able to fit their mannerisms into universal categories of tells. You'll often know exactly what they hold and, better still, you'll know *why* they're acting as they are. You'll get deep inside their minds. And sometimes you'll be positive what cards an opponent holds—just as if he'd turned his hand face up on the table!

When you can do that, your profits will soar. In my opinion, a conscientious winner will at least triple his profits once he masters the science of tells.

It's important that you comprehend the reason why many tells happen. Most tells occur because players are trying to conceal the true strength of their hands. The most likely way they attempt to do this is to act in a manner that will convey the *opposite* of what they're holding. If a hand is weak, they'll try to convince you it's strong. If a hand is strong, they'll try to convince you it's weak. In this sense, your opponents are actors.

This brings us to...

### Caro's Great Law of Tells
*Players are either acting or they aren't. If they are acting, then decide what they want you to do and disappoint them.*

Remember, keep a cool, disinterested attitude. You should be as eager to find a reason to pass as you should be to call. Concentrate and let the tells talk.

When you graduate from this tells course, you'll know for sure why this man...

***Photo 3:***
*... is never as much of a threat...*

*Photo 4:*
*...as this man.*

# HOW TO READ THIS BOOK

The tells discussed in this book follow a disciplined format. It looks like this:

**PHOTO:**
Study the corresponding photo.

**TITLE:**
A label to give you an idea of what the tell is about.

**CATEGORY:**
Provides the type of tell.

**DESCRIPTION:**
Explains what the photo shows.

**MOTIVATION:**
The player's reason for acting the way he does.

**RELIABILITY:**
Weak players = [ ]%
Average players = [ ]%
Strong players = [ ]%

**Reliability** is a rough educated guess, based on several studies and much personal judgment, that shows how often a tell is likely to be accurate. Keep in mind that it does not need to be, and seldom is, 100%.

Tells give you indications which you should balance against all other factors. For instance, if you get a medium-strong tell that your opponent is bluffing, *but he never bluffs,* you have a problem. You should give value to the fact that an opponent never bluffs, but you should also give value to the fact that he seems to be bluffing. One thing that's for certain: He's *more likely to* be bluffing when you see the tell than when you don't.

To be successful at the science of tells, you must always rate the **reliability** in relation to the situation at hand. It's interesting to note that a tell does not need to be even 50 % accurate to be of value! Suppose the pot was $400 and it cost you only $100 to call. Suppose further that you could beat a bluff and *only* a bluff. If this situation occurred five times and you called every time, you'd need to catch your opponent bluffing only once to break even. That's because you'd lose $100 four times (total $400) and once you'd win the $400 that's in the pot. In other words, you'd need to win only 20% of the time. Then, if a tell led you to believe there was a 40% chance your opponent were bluffing, it would certainly be worth a call.

Some tells are nearly 100% accurate. Others are simply powerful clues you should use along with other factors to make your decision.

## VALUE PER HOUR:
$1 limit = $[  ]
$10 limit = $[  ]
$100 limit = $[  ]

**Value Per Hour** provides a very rough figure of how much the tell is worth to you in various size games. The assumption is that you're playing against mostly weak-to-average opponents. You can't just add the value of all the tells together to get an hourly value, because many of them won't exist, and some—when they do exist—will overlap other tells simultaneously occurring and have diminished value. Consider these estimates rough guesses of how much a particular tell will be worth to you if it exists among many opponents in the same game, if you catch it consistently, and apply it correctly.

Tells would tend to be worth more than estimated for me personally—and for other experts—but much less for inexperienced players who don't easily spot them or correctly read them. In fact, the tells will have questionable value even for those who do easily spot them and correctly read them, but who incorrectly apply them!

Consider the estimates to have more meaning if you compare them to estimates for other tells to gauge relative importance than if you try to rely on the exact dollar amount.

## DISCUSSION:

Provides more insight into the tell.

## BEST STRATEGY:

Tells you what to do.

## PLAY-BY-PLAY (WHERE ADDED):

A new category that provides a related example of how you can profitably apply the tell. These new play-by-play examples were added selectively throughout and add significant value because of the provided guidance on how to actually use tells. Play-by-play examples all use MCU Poker Charts (previously called CASM Charts—short for Caro Ante to Showdown Method). For an explanation on how to read these charts, see the next chapter.

# USING MCU
# POKER CHARTS

I devised MCU Poker Charts because there was clearly a need for a common method of presenting poker hands in printed form and on the Web. These charts are designed to be read from left to right and top to bottom, just like you're reading this book.

Actions take place in sequence. So, wherever you see a wager, a fold, or cards appearing, that's when it happened. Everything in the chart that appears earlier—reading left to right, top to bottom—happened earlier. Everything that appears later—reading left to right, top to bottom— happened later.

For your convenience, each MCU Poker Chart has a legend at the bottom, briefly explaining how to interpret it, in case you forget. We'll use three flavors of MCU Poker Charts in this book—one each for hold 'em, seven-card stud, and draw poker.

On the next pages are examples of each of these charts, beginning with hold 'em.

## MCU Poker Chart

**Game:** Hold 'em **Structure:** $25 and $50 blinds, $50 bets on starting hand and flop, $100 thereafter.

| *1* | 2 | 3 | 4 | 5 | 6 | 7 | 8 | 9 | 10 | Pot |
|---|---|---|---|---|---|---|---|---|---|---|
| J♠J / 10♦10 | | ● | b25 | b50 | | | | | | $75 Starting hands <<< |
| | | | | | ▶— | — | — | — | — | |
| =50[1] =100[5] | =100[2] | =100[3] | — | =100[4] | | | | | | $425 |
| | | | | | | | | | | **Flop** J♣J / J♥J / 2♠2 <<< $575 |
| ✓[6] =50[7] | 50 | =50 | | ▶✓ — | | | | | | $575 |
| | | | | | | | | | | **Turn** K♥K <<< $775 |
| ▶✓[8] 10 =100 | ✓ —◀ | 100[9] | | | | | | | | $775 |
| | | | | | | | | | | **River** 7♣7 <<< $1,175 |
| ▶✓ =200[11] | | 100 =200[12]◀ | | | | | | | | $1,175 |
| J♠J / 10♦10 WIN | | K♦K / Q♦Q | | | | | | | | Two-card hands revealed <<< |

20

> **Chart key:** Action reads left to right, top to bottom. Each betting round begins ▶ with and ends with ◀ . Other markings and symbols: a (ante); b (blind bet); ✔ (check); = (call); ▲ (raise); – (fold); ● (dealer position, a.k.a. "the button"). A seat number surrounded by asterisks (for example, *1*) is your seat. Any wager not preceded by a symbol is a voluntary first bet. Wagers indicate the total invested on a betting round. The money in the rightmost column indicates total pot size after the betting.

Here's a fuller explanation. At the top, you see what kind of game we're playing and the betting structure. On the next row, you see the seat numbers. If a number is surrounded by asterisks, such as "*1*" above, that's the seat on which we're focusing our strategy. Often, we will expose the facedown cards for this hand and not for the others until later in the strategy discussion. Private, hidden cards have a line beneath (underline) to differentiate them from exposed cards.

Below the seat numbers is the starting hands row. You can see that this is a full table, because everyone received cards. We're in seat #1, so we see only those cards.

The ● indicates that the #3 seat has the dealer button, so wagers begin to the right with a small $25 blind, marked "b25" and a $50 big blind, marked "b50." Still reading left to right in the starting-hand action row (see rightmost column for description of betting round), you see ▶ in seat #6, meaning the voluntary action on this round starts here. After the starting arrow, you see a dash (—), meaning the player folded. You can always look upward from the bottom in any column. Where you see the dash, that's where the player exited the pot. You see nothing in the betting round columns beneath that fold indicator.

Seats #7, #8, #9, and #10 also fold (note the dashes). Now we skip down to the next line (just like reading a book, remember, left to right, top to bottom). Your seat, #1, says "=50[1]" and is interpreted this way: The equal sign means call, the "50" indicates the amount (equal to the big blind), and the superscript [1] means that you should look for that number in the comments following the table (omitted here) to see what is said about the strategy at that point in the action.

Seat #2 is marked " ▲ 100[2]"—and this means the player raised to a total of $100 for the betting round (a $50 raise) and that a strategy note (number 2) follows the chart. The rest of the action in this betting round, I'm sure you can follow. The ◀ symbol follows the very last action on the betting round. The cumulative size of the pot at the end of the betting round is shown last in the rightmost column. Here it's $425. The pot size, after the betting, is provided for every betting round.

Now we move down to the second betting round, the action on the flop. First you see the flop over in the right hand column. Then comes the wagering. The only thing you need to know here is that a check mark ( ✔ ) means that the player checked.

The betting round following the fourth communal board card ("Turn") and the final one ("River") are shown in separate rows. On the bottom row, you see the showdown to determine the winner—and the winning hand is indicated with the word, "WIN." (Those adopting the MCU Poker Charts can also use the bottom row to expose, for instructive purposes, other hands that did not reach the showdown. These should be marked as non-showdown hands, such as by including the word "FOLDED" at the bottom. These non-showdown private cards can also be revealed in the text following the table or they can be shown exposed in the table, instead of concealed, as they are dealt. The method used should be the one that is most useful for the purpose.)

Again, the strategy notes that correspond to the superscripts are not relevant for this example, and are not included here. In the charts used in conjunction with the tells in this book, any superscript numbers have corresponding explanations following the chart.

Optionally, the areas on the chart pertaining to a player's actions can be shaded for betting rounds after a hand is folded. This makes it easier to see who's still active, and that's the method used in this book.

Now let's look at a seven-card stud MCU Poker Chart...

## MCU Poker Chart

*Game:* Seven-card stud *Structure:* $10 ante, $15 low card forced bring-in bet, $50 bets on starting hand and 4th street, $100 thereafter.

| 1 | 2 | 3 | 4 | 5 | 6 | *7* | 8 | Pot |
|---|---|---|---|---|---|---|---|---|
| a10 | a10 | a10 | a10 | a10 | a10 | a10 / 8♦8 / K♣K | a10 | $80 — Starting hands <<< |
| Q♦Q / — | 3♦3 / ▸b15 / — | 4♣4 / =15 / =100[3] | 9♦9 / — | 10♦10 / =15 / =100[4] | 7♥7 / — | 8♠8 / ▲50[1] / =100[5] | J♠J / ▲100[2] | $495 |
| | | Q♥Q / ▸✔ / — | | J♦J / ✔ / =50 | | 6♥6 / ✔ / =50◂ | 7♠7 / 50[6] | 4th Street <<< $645 |
| | | | | Q♣Q / =100◂ | | 6♥6 / ▸100[7] | 2♥2 / =100[8] | 5th Street <<< $945 |
| | | | | 5♥5 / ✔◂ | | A♣A / ▸✔[9] | A♠A / ✔ | 6th Street <<< $945 |
| | | | | =50 / ▲200 | | K♦K / ▸100[10] / =200◂[11] | — | River <<< $1,345 |
| | | | | 10♥10 / 2♠2 / 10♣10 / WIN | | 8♦8 / K♣K / K♦K | | Hole cards revealed (river card last) <<< |

> **Chart key:** Action reads left to right, top to bottom. Each betting round begins ▶ with and ends with ◀ . Other markings and symbols: a (ante); b (blind bet); ✔ (check); = (call); ▲ (raise); – (fold); ● (dealer position, a.k.a. "the button"). A seat number surrounded by asterisks (for example, *1*) is your seat. Any wager not preceded by a symbol is a voluntary first bet. Wagers indicate the total invested on a betting round. The money in the rightmost column indicates total pot size after the betting.

Now that we've walked through the hold 'em chart together, you probably already understand how to read this seven-card stud version. Because there are no communal cards, each player's cards are individual and appear as they are dealt.

The "a10" stands for $10 ante. The "b15" stands for the forced low-card "bring-in" bet (or "blind" if you prefer).

And, finally, we use five-card draw (both high and low) MCU Poker Charts. Here's one for five-card draw...

## MCU Poker Chart

**Game:** Jacks-or-better draw, joker added  **Structure:** $5 ante, $25 bets before draw, $50 after.

| 1 | 2 | 3 | 4 | 5 | 6 | *7* | 8 | Pot |
|---|---|---|---|---|---|---|---|---|
| a5 | a5 | a5 | a5 | a5 | a5 | a5 | a5 | $40 |
|  |  |  |  |  |  | K♠ K |  |  |
|  |  |  |  |  |  | K♥ K |  | Hands before the draw <<< |
|  |  |  |  |  |  | A♠ A |  |  |
|  |  |  |  |  |  | 2♠ 2 |  |  |
|  |  |  |  |  |  | Joker |  |  |
|  |  |  | ● | ▶✔ | ✔ | 25 |  |  |
| =25 | – | – | ▲50 | – |  | =50[1] | – |  |
| – ◀ |  |  |  |  |  |  |  | $165 |

| | | | 1◀ card | | ▶1 card (dis- card 2♠²) | | |
|---|---|---|---|---|---|---|---|
| | | | ▦ ▦ ▦ ▦ + ▦ | | K♠ K / K♥ K / A♠ A / Joker / + / 4♠ 4 | | The draw <<< |
| | | | ♠100 | | ▶50¹ =100◀ | | After the draw <<< $365 |
| | | | A♥ A / 9♥ 9 / 4♥ 4 / 3♥ 3 / 2♥ 2 WIN | | K♠ K / K♥ K / A♠ A / Joker / 4♠ 4 | | Hands revealed <<< |

**Chart key:** Action reads left to right, top to bottom. Each betting round begins ▶ with and ends with ◀ . Other markings and symbols: a (ante); b (blind bet); ✔ (check); = (call); ♠ (raise); – (fold); ● (dealer position, a.k.a. "the button"). A seat number surrounded by asterisks (for example, *1*) is your seat. Any wager not preceded by a symbol is a voluntary first bet. Wagers indicate the total invested on a betting round. The money in the rightmost column indicates total pot size after the betting.

By now, the previous chart also should be fairly easy to understand. The starting hands are shown as they are dealt before the first round of betting. Then you see the cards kept, followed by a + sign below. That + sign separates the cards held from the new cards received on the draw. Put together, the cards above the + sign and the cards below it (if any) constitute the final hand held. The showdown, if present, appears in the row below the final betting.

## OTHER DETAILS

MCU Poker Charts don't require the graphical cards shown above. You can substitute other graphics or text symbols to define a card. So you can, alternatively, present a starting hand like this: J♠ 10♦.

Those symbols don't need to be used, if unavailable. Substitutions may be needed on web sites, for instance. In such cases, these are the sanctioned changes:

- Use * instead of ● for the dealer-position button.
- Use > instead of ▶ to indicate the first voluntary action.
- Use < instead of ◀ to indicate the last action on the betting round.
- Use r instead of ▲ to indicate a raise or reraise.
- Use k instead of ✔ to indicate a check.
- Use -- (two hyphens) instead of — (typographical dash) to indicate a fold.
- Use  c d h s instead of ♣♦♥♠, if the card symbols are unavailable.
- Use (1), (2), (3), and so forth, instead of [1], [2], [3] (superscripts) to indicate places in the action that match comments following the MCU Poker Chart.

The table format, with bordered rows and columns, should be maintained. This is standard fare for the web as well as almost all word processors.

## IT'S FREE TO EVERYONE

Finally, I have given the concept and the design for these MCU Poker Charts to the public. I am not claiming any rights to them. Anyone can use them. I hope they become universally accepted. I also hope nobody changes the concept or the specific way information is presented. There may be ways to improve these charts, but if everyone goes their own way, we won't have a universal way of communicating poker strategy. And we need one.

There is also a Type II MCU Poker Chart (the one we're using is Type I) that I won't describe in detail here. It depicts a clockwise spiral pathway leading toward the pot at center. Superimposed on the spiral is a geometric "pie" with each slice representing a poker seat. All the action takes place in order, within the appropriate player slices, including wagers and cards received, as you mentally travel along the spiral toward the pot. It is worthy of future use, but deemed too cumbersome to employ in this book.

I'm open to suggestions for future improvement in the MCU Poker Chart standard. Any improvements accepted will be formally announced periodically, and none should be so radical that people reading older charts cannot easily understand the new ones. This is my dream. I hope other publishers adopt MCU Poker Charts as their standard, that they comment freely on the design, and that they become a part of the team behind this minor improvement in our united effort to popularize poker worldwide.

*Note: Publishers, instructors, and others wanting to adopt the MCU Poker Charts as a standard can find Microsoft Word templates at www.planetpoker.com.*

# "CARO'S LAW OF LOOSE WIRING" AND POKER TELLS

First I'm going to share a secret with you. Then we'll put our heads together and figure out what it has to do with poker tells. The secret is so powerful that it applies to real-life situations you encounter many times each day. It has special importance to poker generally and to tells specifically—as we'll see later.

First, let's look at a version—specially edited for this book with MCU Poker Charts included—of something I wrote for Card Player magazine early in 1999. The heading was...

### "Caro's Law of Loose Wiring"— Possibly Poker's Least Understood Concept

I've been talking about this concept for a long, long time, but few people seem to understand its significance. In fact, many players tend to plot strategy as if the phenomenon I'm about to discuss didn't exist.

I'm talking about Caro's Law of Loose Wiring. It's an extremely important law, but you'll have to trust me when I tell you that it's worthwhile for you to wade through this discussion. Eventually, this will all make sense. But first, we need to look at two separate hold 'em pots, beginning with the blinds and following through until the showdown.

## POT A
### $75/$150 hold 'em

Betting round one: Seat #1 puts in $50 small blind; seat #2 puts in $75 big blind; seat #3 raises to $150; seat #4 folds; seat #5 calls $150; seat #6 reraises to $225; seat #7 folds; seat #8 folds; seat #9 folds; seat #1 calls to $225; seat #2 folds; seat #3 calls to $225; seat #5 calls to $225.

Four players stay for $225, making the pot $975, including the surrendered big blind.

Flop is...

Betting round two: Seat #1 checks; seat #3 bets $75 (a questionable, but aggressive and not unusual bet, as you'll see); seat #5 calls $75 (a weak but not unusual call); seat #6 raises to $150; seat #1 reraises to $225; seat #3 folds; seat #5 calls to $225 (perhaps in desperation—who knows?); seat #6 caps the betting by making it $300—the final legal raise; seat #1 calls to $300; seat #5 calls to $300.

Three players remain. Add it up and it's another $975 round. The pot is now $1,950.

Turn card is...

making the board

Betting round three: Seat #1 checks; seat #5 bets $150 (betting limits have doubled); seat #6 calls $150; seat #1 hesitates, seems about to fold, seems about to call, then suddenly raises to $300; seat #5 reraises to $450; seat #6 calls to $450; seat #1 calls to $450.

Three players still remain. The pot is now $3,300. River card is...

making the final board

Final round betting: Seat #1 checks; seat #5 bets $150; seat #6 raises to $300; seat #1 folds; seat #5 calls to $300.

There is a showdown between seat #5 and seat #6 to determine the winner of Pot A. Seat #6 wins the pot, which is $3,900. I'm not going to tell you what those showdown cards were just yet. First we need to look at the one more pot.

### POT B
#### $75/$150 hold 'em

I'll just give you the short version of this pot, so we can get straight to the point.

Betting round one: Seat #1 puts in $50 small blind; seat #2 puts in $75 big blind; seat #3 raises to $150; seat #4 folds; seat #5 folds; seat #6 folds; seat #7 calls $150; seat #8 folds; seat #9 folds; seat #1 folds; seat #2 (the big blind) calls to $150 ($75 more).

Three players stay for $150, making the pot $500, including the surrendered small blind. This time the Pot B fighting before the flop is among seat #2, seat #3, and seat

#7. Pot A's fighting before the flop was among seat #1, seat #3, seat #5, and seat #6.

Flop is...

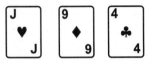

same as in Pot A.

Betting round two: Everyone checks.

Three players remain. The pot is still $500.

Turn card is...

making the board...

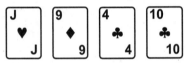

The odds against any next two consecutive flops and turn cards being the same, by the way, are 1,082,899 to 1. There are flop-turn combinations that are effectively the same, with different suits, however. For instance...

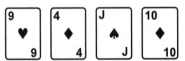

would be the same board from a logical point of view, assuming you know nothing about the secret cards of the players. Anyway, where was I?

Betting round three: Seat #2 checks; seat #3 checks; seat #7 bets $150; seat #2 folds; seat #3 calls $150.

It's heads up between seat #3 and seat #7. The pot is now $800.

River card is...

Talk about magic! It took me a long time to learn how to do that trick. So, again, the final board is...

Final round betting: Seat #3 checks; seat #7 bets $150; seat #3 folds. There is no showdown, and seat #7 captures the $950 pot, including his uncalled final $150 wager.

### Hands Exposed

Now let's expose the two-card starting hands held by the players in Pot A:

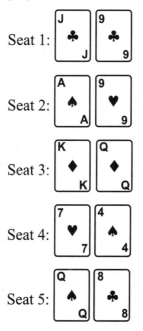

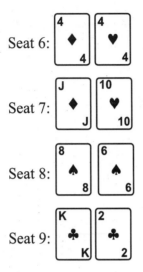

Seat 6: 4♦ 4♥

Seat 7: J♦ 10♥

Seat 8: 8♠ 6♠

Seat 9: K♣ 2♣

Before you read further, go back over the action with this new knowledge. Let's use an MCU Poker Chart to make it easier to review the action. I'll do you a favor by showing all the private cards face up before the flop...

**MCU Poker Chart**

*Game:* Hold 'em *Structure:* $50 and $75 blinds, $75 bets on starting hand and flop, $150 thereafter.

| 1 | 2 | 3 | 4 | 5 | 6 | 7 | 8 | 9 | 10 | Pot |
|---|---|---|---|---|---|---|---|---|----|-----|
| b50 | b75 | | | | | | | ● | | $125 |
| J♣/J | A♦/A | K♥/K | 7♥/7 | Q♠/Q | 4♥/4 | J♦/J | 8♠/8 | K♣/K | | **Starting hands** |
| 9♣/9 | 9♥/9 | Q♦/Q | 4♠/4 | 8♣/8 | 4♦/4 | 10♥/10 | 6♠/6 | 2♣/2 | | <<< |
| =225 | — | ▲150 =225 | — | =150 =225◄ | ▲225 | — | — | — | | $975 |

**Flop**: J♥/J 9♦/9 4♣/4  <<< $1,950

| 1 | 2 | 3 | 4 | 5 | 6 | 7 | 8 | 9 | 10 | Pot |
|---|---|---|---|---|---|---|---|---|----|-----|
| ▶✓ ▲225 =300 | | 75 — | | =75 =225 =300◄ | ▲150 ▲300 | | | | | $1,950 |

**Turn**: 10♣/10  <<< $3,300

| 1 | 2 | 3 | 4 | 5 | 6 | 7 | 8 | 9 | 10 | Pot |
|---|---|---|---|---|---|---|---|---|----|-----|
| ▶✓ ▲300 =450◄ | | | | 150 ▲450 | =150 =450 | | | | | $3,300 |

**River**: 10♠/10  <<< $3,900

| 1 | 2 | 3 | 4 | 5 | 6 | 7 | 8 | 9 | 10 | Pot |
|---|---|---|---|---|---|---|---|---|----|-----|
| ▶✓ — | | | | =150 =300◄ | ▲300 | | | | | $3,900 |

**Two-card hands revealed** <<<

| 1 | 2 | 3 | 4 | 5 | 6 | 7 | 8 | 9 | 10 | Pot |
|---|---|---|---|---|---|---|---|---|----|-----|
| | | | | Q♠/Q 8♣/8 | 4♥/4 4♦/4 WIN | | | | | |

**Chart key:** Action reads left to right, top to bottom. Each betting round begins ▶ with and ends with ◄ . Other markings and symbols: a (ante); b (blind bet); ✓ (check); = (call); ▲ (raise); – (fold); ● (dealer position, a.k.a. "the button"). A seat number surrounded by asterisks (for example, *1*) is your seat. Any wager not preceded by a symbol is a voluntary first bet. Wagers indicate the total invested on a betting round. The money in the rightmost column indicates total pot size after the betting.

Examine the previous MCU Poker Chart and you'll see some weak calls, maybe an unexpected raise or two, and several borderline decisions. Yes, many of your opponents really do play hands this way—quite often!

OK, now let's look at the two-card starting hands held by players in Pot B:

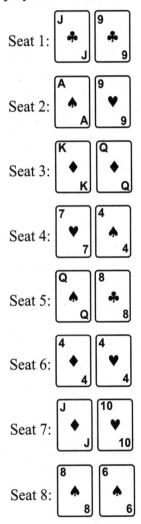

Seat 1: J♣ 9♣

Seat 2: A♠ 9♥

Seat 3: K♦ Q♦

Seat 4: 7♥ 4♠

Seat 5: Q♠ 8♣

Seat 6: 4♦ 4♥

Seat 7: J♦ 10♥

Seat 8: 8♠ 6♠

Seat 9: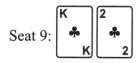

Ah, gee whiz! They typeset the same hands again. Let me go talk to all the printer-publisher-type people and see if we can get it straightened out. I'll be right back with the Pot B hands…

## LOOSE WIRING EXPLAINED

My mistake. Those really were the Pot B hands. But it gets weirder. In fact, not only did every single player have exactly the same cards, rank for rank and suit for suit, but both pots had identical flops, turns, and rivers! Talk about a long shot—I don't think I've ever seen that before.

Here's an MCU Poker Chart for Hand B…

## MCU Poker Chart

**Game:** Hold 'em **Structure:** $50 and $75 blinds, $75 bets on starting hand and flop, $150 thereafter.

| 1 | 2 | 3 | 4 | 5 | 6 | 7 | 8 | 9 | 10 | Pot |
|---|---|---|---|---|---|---|---|---|----|-----|
| b50 | b75 | | | | | | | ● | | $125 |
| J♣ J | A♠ A | K♦ K | 7♥ 7 | Q♠ Q | 4♥ 4 | J♦ J | 8♠ 8 | K♣ K | | **Starting hands** <<< |
| 9♣ 9 | 9♥ 9 | Q♦ Q | 4♠ 4 | 8♣ 8 | 4♦ 4 | 10♥ 10 | 6♦ 6 | 2♣ 2 | | |
| | | ▶150 | — | — | — | =150 | — | — | | $500 |
| — | =150◀ | | | | | | | | | |
| | | | | | | | | | | **Flop** J♥ J / 9♦ 9 / 4♣ 4 <<< $500 |
| | | ▶✔ | ✔ | | | | ✔◀ | | | $500 |
| | | | | | | | | | | **Turn** 10♣ 10 <<< $800 |
| | | ▶✔ — | ✔ =150◀ | | | | 150 | | | $800 |
| | | | | | | | | | | **River** 10♠ 10 <<< $950 |
| | | ▶✔ —◀ | | | | | 150 WIN | | | $950 |

**Chart key:** Action reads left to right, top to bottom. Each betting round begins ▶ with and ends with ◀. Other markings and symbols: a (ante); b (blind bet); ✔ (check); = (call); ▲ (raise); – (fold); ● (dealer position, a.k.a. "the button"). A seat number surrounded by asterisks (for example, *1*) is your seat. Any wager not preceded by a symbol is a voluntary first bet. Wagers indicate the total invested on a betting round. The money in the rightmost column indicates total pot size after the betting.

Those two hands demonstrate *Caro's Law of Loose Wiring…*

> ### Caro's Law of Loose Wiring
> *"If choices are not clearly connected to their benefits, people usually interact in ways that make outcomes unpredictable. If choices are clearly connected to their benefits, people sometimes act in ways that make outcomes unpredictable."*

You see, your poker opponents are volatile beings. They can be impressionable, irritable, playful, capricious, and more. You don't know when they're going to short out, cross-circuit, or do the silliest or the most brilliant things. This goes for all poker players, from the weakest beginners to the most seasoned pros.

The deal is that even when opponents are playing a disciplined game of poker, so many of their decisions are borderline that what they're going to do is anybody's guess. In the example hands, we not only ended up with a different group of main players, we ended up with a different winner. And we ended up with one pot almost $4,000 and one pot under $1,000. And it all makes perfect sense, when you think about it.

One more thing, just so I can really drive home the importance of *Caro's Law of Loose Wiring.* These were all the same players in the same environment feeling the same emotions up until the moment they acted! All I did was wipe the first pot from their memories and have them play it over again.

## THE TRUTH ABOUT POKER PLAYERS

Here's what I want you to know:

**1)** Most hands your opponents play are at whim! That's because there are relatively few overwhelmingly strong or weak hands that dictate an exact tactic.

**2)** Some hands your opponents play at whim are the result of spontaneous decisions about whether to fold, call, or raise!

**3)** Your opponents' habits of playing a large spectrum of hands at whim is not necessarily bad for them! Sometimes it can be closely in tune with game theory and can cause them to "randomize" their decisions effectively.

**4)** When you try to analyze poker strategy, you need to realize that you simply can't say how most opponents would play a hand or—in many cases —*if* they would have played a hand. They often don't know this themselves until the very last second!

**5)** If you're an accomplished player profiting from the flow of the game, many of *your* play-or-don't-play decisions are made by whim at the last moment!

**6)** Your decisions made by whim at the last moment are not necessarily bad for you, either!

## MAKING THEIR WHIM WORK FOR YOU

When you glue these truths together, you begin to understand poker in a way that will never be possible if you think of it like a chess match. You will begin to see why actions and responses are so volatile in poker. And you will begin to know that opponents are often looking for anything to direct their borderline decisions this way or that.

Yes, they are deciding by whim, but it's your job to make their whim work for you. You need to understand how readily opponents can be influenced by what you say and how you behave. And then you can take poker to the final level.

And from that powerful lesson, explaining *Caro's Law of Loose Wiring,* we can begin to comprehend the importance of tells. Since so many poker opponents often decide at whim, we need to do more than just strategically analyze their actions relative to what they *should be* doing. We need to watch and listen and determine what they *are* doing.

# TELLS FROM THOSE
# WHO ARE UNAWARE

When I get through with you, the magic of tells will be your key to profit for life. Most of your profit will come from reading players who are trying to deceive you. Those are actors who are aware of what they're doing. Usually they will act exactly opposite of the true strength of their cards. If their hands are hideous, they will try to make you think that they hold something fearsome. If their hands are powerful, they will try to convince you that they hold garbage. We'll get into the world of actors in *Chapter 6—Tells From Actors.*

Right now we'll deal with another important category of tells. The folks in the upcoming photos will give you valuable information, even though they *won't* be trying to fool you.

Although these tells are not from actors, these same people probably *will be* actors at other times. It's just that they aren't bothering to act at this particular moment. So let's see what they have to tell us...

# Noncombat Tells

While the majority of tells occur during the competition for a poker pot, there is some valuable information that can be learned about our opponents when they're not involved in a poker hand.

Poker tests our perception. It also tests our logic and our competitive instincts. In a sense it's a safe and sane form of warfare. Poker war is not only the competition for each pot, hand after hand. Poker war is bigger than just *hand-to-hand* combat, because there are important things happening *between* hands—things you should be observing.

Besides the noncombat tells illustrated in this section, you should notice things about each player's appearance that might provide clues to future poker behavior.

Specifically, well-dressed people tend to play conservatively. However, a man wearing a rumpled business suit with a loosened tie is probably in a gambling mood and will play looser than he would if that same suit were recently donned and his tie were in perfect position.

Poker authority John Fox claims that people wearing religious amulets are luck conscious, hard to bluff and play too many pots. Obviously the Reverend Fox means no disrespect with that theory, and there is probably truth in it. Certainly, players displaying good-luck charms or showing superstitious behavior tend to be more liberal with their poker dollars than average players.

Here are a few of my personal observations and those of my students. (Many of those students have been women and minorities, so in no sense are these comments intended as sexist, racist or unfriendly.) As a general rule, women are harder to bluff than men. Orientals are either very skillful or very luck oriented. Relatively few blacks play to win; most tend to gamble more liberally than other players. When you're up against an unknown player, you'll earn extra profit by assuming he or she will play as a stereotype until you learn differently.

Let's look at some noncombat tells…

# TELL #1

### TITLE:
When I was a boy, I liked to play with blocks.

### CATEGORY:
Noncombat

### DESCRIPTION:
This man has gone out of his way to arrange his chips neatly. He's even bothered to line up the markings on the sides of the chips.

### MOTIVATION:
His personality, be it permanent or momentary, is not reckless. Neatly arranged chips make him feel secure.

### RELIABILITY:
Weak players = 88%
Average players = 68%
Strong players = 59%

### VALUE PER HOUR:
$1 limit = $0.33
$10 limit = $1.14
$100 limit = $3.15

### DISCUSSION:
Very rarely is stacking chips used as a ploy by a player. Most players only bother to act when the rewards are immediate (i.e., a pot which is still being fought for). Glimpses of an opponent's true nature can often be gained by watching the way he stacks his chips. The very organized manner in which these chips are arranged suggests that this

player will probably choose his hands carefully, seldomly bluff and won't display a lot of gamble.

Of course his mood may change during the game, but in that case his stacks will probably become less neatly arranged. Notice that there are a few extra chips on top of his large stacks. This could be his profit. That's important to know, because you can frequently bluff successfully just by betting slightly more than his profit.

Players are reluctant to call when they're winning, but would be losing if they made an unsuccessful call. Also, note that this fellow is very neatly attired. This is often, but not always, an indication of conservative play.

## BEST STRATEGY:

Don't get involved with medium-strength hands after this man has entered a pot. Bluff him somewhat more often than you would other players. Don't call as liberally when he bets.

*Photo 5:*
*Does neatness count?*

# TELL #2

## TITLE:
Building code violations.

## CATEGORY:
Noncombat.

## DESCRIPTION:
This player isn't terribly concerned about how his chips appear. They are unarranged and uncountable.

## MOTIVATION:
The player feels like gambling, is poised for action and is not thinking about real money.

## RELIABILITY:
Weak players = 79%
Average players = 62%
Strong players = 53%

## VALUE PER HOUR:
$1 limit = $0.27
$10 limit = $0.90
$100 limit = $2.70

## DISCUSSION:
Although players will sometimes fool you, haphazardly stacked chips usually mean careless play. This player's game will probably be too liberal, but he might also get good value from his big hands by playing aggressively. There's a good chance this man is prepared to lose all those chips, and often he will.

## BEST STRATEGY:

Call more often when he bets. Bluff him less frequently than other players.

---

### Caro's Law of Tells #1
*Players often stack chips in a manner directly indicative of their style of play. Conservative means conservative; sloppy means sloppy.*

---

*Photo 6:*
*This man doesn't seem to care how many chips he has.*

# TELL # 3

## TITLE:
Help, hurry, I want to gamble!

## CATEGORY:
Noncombat.

## DESCRIPTION:
The man at left is out of chips and he wants more. He's making sure he gets immediate attention by waving his money in the air.

## MOTIVATION:
This guy doesn't mind letting people know that, at least temporarily, he has money to gamble with. Often he's compensating for the "humiliation" of having lost his chips by making certain everyone knows he isn't broke. He may even feel playful in anticipation of gambling more freely than before. It's rare for a conservative player to use a flamboyant method of buying chips to fool you; that is unusual among weak or average players.

## RELIABILITY:
Weak players = 75 %
Average players = 72%
Strong players = 55%

## VALUE PER HOUR:
$1 limit = $0.24
$10 limit = $0.75
$100 limit = $20

## DISCUSSION:

Even though this tell isn't always accurate, when a man asks for chips in a flamboyant manner, there's a much better chance that he's going to play aggressively and often carelessly.

## BEST STRATEGY:

Until you know differently, treat this man as you would any other loose player. Call more often; bluff less often.

*Photo 7:*
*This man is asking for chips and wants it to be known.*

# TELL #4

## TITLE:
Where is that $100 I hid here in 1976?

## CATEGORY:
Noncombat.

## DESCRIPTION:
This man is buying chips, but doesn't want anyone to see what is in his wallet.

## MOTIVATION:
He is by nature conservative about money. It's possible that he doesn't have much money in his wallet and is embarrassed to show it. Maybe he has a lot of money in his wallet and doesn't want anyone to see it. The general truth is that he simply isn't a flashy player.

## RELIABILITY:
Weak players = 80%
Average players = 65 %
Strong players = 60%

## VALUE PER HOUR:
$1 limit = $0.15
$10 limit = $0.33
$100 limit = $0.90

## DISCUSSION:
This is exactly the opposite of the previous tell. When you see a player hiding his bankroll, there's a very good chance he'll play conservatively. Usually he won't even

lift his wallet above the table to buy chips. He'll guard it in his lap.

## BEST STRATEGY:

Call him less; bluff him more.

---

### Caro's Law of Tells #2

*Players often buy chips in a manner directly indicative of their style of play. Flamboyant means flamboyant; guarded means guarded.*

---

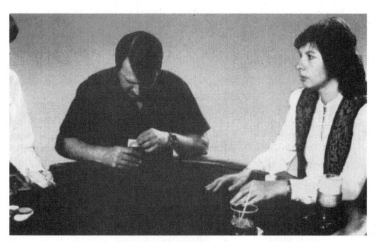

### Photo 8:

*This man is squeezing money from his wallet to buy chips.*

# TELL #5

**TITLE:**

I bet I can wait longer than you can.

**CATEGORY:**

Noncombat.

**DESCRIPTION:**

From the expression on this player's face, his mind seems to be on something other than poker. He's leaning back slumped with his arms folded.

**MOTIVATION:**

This player is not in a gambling mood and is simply relaxing while waiting patiently for a good poker hand.

**RELIABILITY:**

Weak players = 90%
Average players = 85 %
Strong players = 78%

**VALUE PER HOUR:**

$1 limit = $0.30
$10 limit = $0.54
$100 limit = $1.32

**DISCUSSION:**

This sort of body language seems to convey patience and that's exactly right. Here you see that this player has just received his fourth card in seven stud. He apparently has little interest in this pot. It's possible he got the fourth card for free because nobody bet on third street. In any case, this pot isn't very important to him. Players who are winning and wish to sit on their lead will often simply lean back and wait for the good opportunities. True, players often *act* uninterested when they have strong hands, but that isn't the case here. If this man were trying to deceive you, he'd probably do more than just lean back and stare. He'd likely look away from the action or even start to throw his hand away prematurely. Those tells will be analyzed later. Take a good look at this man. When you see someone whose mannerisms are similar, you can be pretty sure he'll play only quality hands.

**BEST STRATEGY:**

Seldom get involved in a pot with this man.

***Photo 9:***
*This man is leaning back with his
arms folded, relaxing.*

# TELL #6

## TITLE:
I've got better things to do than play poker.

## CATEGORY:
Noncombat.

## DESCRIPTION:
Again we see a player leaning back and looking uninterested. This time he is not folding his arms.

## MOTIVATION:
He is feeling patient.

## RELIABILITY:
Weak players = 88%
Average players = 78%
Strong players = 68%

## VALUE PER HOUR:
$1 limit = $0.24
$10 limit = $0.51
$100 limit = $1.05

## DISCUSSION:
This is similar to the previous tell. However, when a player has his arms folded, he's generally in a long-range waiting mode. Some players lean slightly forward when they're interested in a hand and otherwise (as in this photo) slump backward. Players may even be aware that they're doing this, but it's too much effort for them to try to camouflage their behavior—especially when they figure

nobody is watching for it.

## BEST STRATEGY:

If you act before this player, play some slightly weaker hands which you would normally pass. That's because this player is no threat to you at the moment. He's making it easier for you to steal the antes.

*Photo 10:*
*This player is also leaning back*
*and appears to be patient.*

# TELL #7

## TITLE:
When will I ever get a chance to stack these chips?

## CATEGORY:
Noncombat.

## DESCRIPTION:
There are a great deal of chips scattered in front of the woman. That's not because she isn't organized. It's because she just won a giant pot and hasn't had time to stack it.

## MOTIVATION:
Won last pot.

## RELIABILITY:
Weak players = 85 %
Average players = 80%
Strong players = 74%

## VALUE PER HOUR:
$1 limit = $0.12
$10 limit = $0.27
$100 limit = $0.63

## DISCUSSION:
Most players like to stack their chips before they get involved in another pot. This doesn't mean they won't play strong hands. A player may even toss in a few chips on medium-strength hands as a courtesy while sorting through the last pot. However, there's one thing players will almost never do in this situation, and that's run a bluff from scratch.

True, they may end up bluffing, but when they enter pots, it's almost always because their hands merit it.

## BEST STRATEGY:

If this woman plays a hand while she's still stacking a giant pot, give her credit for having at least medium power. Don't invest money on the hope that she entered the pot bluffing.

***Photo 11:***
*The woman has just won a major pot
and the next hand is beginning.*

# Sharing a Hand

Once in a while a player will show his hand to someone who isn't involved in the pot. The kibitzer can be a fellow player who has already thrown away his hand. Maybe it's a friend or relative who's just approached the table. Sometimes friends sit nearby to watch their favorite poker hero compete.

You'll find fantastic clues to the strength of an opponent's hand when two players are sharing it. If the onlooker has approached while the hand is already in progress, then *he's* the one to watch. He will likely use subtle kindergarten psychology in an attempt to help the poker-playing friend along. For instance, if the kibitzer has arrived in the middle of the hand, he may sigh sadly if what he sees is very strong. If that hand is weak, he may just keep staring at it admiringly. In this sense, the kibitzer will usually act in a manner opposite the strength of the hand he's viewing. Acting strong when weak or weak when strong contributes to many of the tells you'll learn in *Chapter 6—Tells From Actors.*

But when a hand is shared from the very *beginning,* players tend to follow a trend without knowing it. Then they are not actors; they are unaware. Here is the tell I have in mind. . .

# TELL #8

## TITLE:
Let's win this one together, darlin'.

## CATEGORY:
Sharing a Hand.

## DESCRIPTION:
The man at center is competing for this pot. Sometime *after* he became involved, his girlfriend walked up. At that point he decided it was all right to let her see his cards.

## MOTIVATION:
Perhaps he wants her to know he's playing a legitimate hand and is not gambling recklessly. He may also want to impress her with his card-playing ability, feeling pretty confident that his hand is good enough to claim the pot.

## RELIABILITY:
Weak players = 68%
Average players = 65%
Strong players = 55%

## VALUE PER HOUR:
$1 limit = $0.21
$10 limit = $0.60
$100 limit = $0.66

## DISCUSSION:
Usually if a man is involved in a hand that he knows he shouldn't be playing, he will *not* share it with a pal, wife or girlfriend who happens along in the midst of poker combat. If he does share it, it's probable that the hand is strong

enough to merit his investment. If this guy held poor cards or was bluffing, he would likely be afraid to show his hand for two reasons. First, he might unwillingly impress upon the onlooker that he plays poorly. Second, the onlooker might accidentally tip off to his opponents that his hand is weak, costing him the pot. Strong players are less likely to exhibit this tell, and some may even use it as a ploy to attempt a bluff. Against a strong opponent, watch the onlooker for clues.

## BEST STRATEGY:

Don't bet into this player or call him with anything less than a solid hand.

> ### Caro's Law of Tells #3
> *Any unsophisticated player who bets, then shares his hand while awaiting a call, is unlikely to be bluffing.*

*Photo 12:*
*The man at center is letting the woman share his hand.*

# Shuffling a Hand

There are many ways players show their impatience or their anxiety. Many nervous habits can be detected, and rarely is your opponent aware that he's exhibiting these mannerisms.

We'll talk more about this in Section IV, titled *Nervousness*. First, be aware that—particularly in draw poker and occasionally in seven stud— players will shuffle their cards before looking at them. Let's see how it works and what it means...

# TELL #9

**TITLE:**

Don't make me look until I have to.

**CATEGORY:**

Shuffling a Hand.

**DESCRIPTION:**

What you see here happens frequently in five-card draw poker. Imagine that the woman has drawn one card to a flush. She will continue to take the top card from her hand and place it on the bottom. She'll do this over and over until the action reaches her and it's time to look.

**MOTIVATION:**

She needs to improve her hand to win and doesn't want to see how it comes out just yet. Building suspense is a common habit with some players; it usually happens when they figure they don't have the best hand and must therefore get lucky on the draw.

**RELIABILITY:**

Weak players = 79%
Average players = 75%
Strong players = 70%

**VALUE PER HOUR:**

$1 limit = $0.42
$10 limit = $1.50
$100 limit = $3.75

## DISCUSSION:

When you see a player shuffling through his or her cards (usually in draw poker, you should figure the hand requires help.) Also, it turns out that there's a much better than average chance that the player is drawing to an especially powerful hand. In draw lowball, many players shuffle only if they're drawing to a bicycle (5-4-3-2-A, the best possible hand) or a six.

Players seldom shuffle on less suspenseful lowball draws, such as one-card to a nine. In high-hand-wins draw poker, there's a very great chance that any player prolonging the suspense by shuffling his cards is drawing to a straight or a flush (or even a straight flush). Sometimes you'll find seven-stud players shuffling their three hole cards before looking at their seventh (final) card. As you'd expect, among weak players, this generally means they must improve their hand to win.

## BEST STRATEGY:

Use logic. Suppose you're playing jacks-or-better-to open draw poker. You open with a pair of aces. An opponent calls. You draw three; he draws one. You look at your hand and see three aces.

Normally you'd be tempted to bet in this situation, because if your opponent was drawing to two pair and it didn't help (which is likely to happen 11 out of 12 times), he'd probably call you anyway. However, when that opponent is shuffling, you should figure that there's a very good chance he's drawing to a straight or a flush, and you should therefore check rather than bet. If the game is lowball and an opponent draws one, shuffles, then bets, you should *not* raise with a smooth seven (such as 7-4-3-2-A), even though you might have raised had he not shuffled.

***Photo 13:***
*The woman is shuffling her cards before she looks.*
*She slides the top card off...*

***Photo 14:***
*...and puts it on the bottom, then repeats the process.*

# Nervousness

Genuine nervousness is hard to fake. Usually you should interpret it for what it means. Fine, but what does it mean? If a poker player seems nervous, is it because he has a strong hand or because he's bluffing?

Many people suspect that players show more nervousness when they're bluffing. After all, there's a great deal of strain involved when you're bluffing and you know everyone's attention is focused on you. Some players are so scared when they bluff that they scarcely breathe.

So, are players with weak hands more likely to show nervousness than players with strong hands? Usually not! And especially not in limit poker. In no-limit games where the strain of bluffing into a large pot can bring genuine nervousness to the surface, you could argue that players are more likely to remain calm when they have a big hand than when they're bluffing.

Not true. Even in no-limit poker, there's an overwhelming tendency for players to *appear* calm when they're bluffing. In a sense, it's an act, so maybe we should include this discussion in *Chapter 6—Tells From Actors.* But disguising nervousness by conveying calm is not always a conscious act. Often it's something a player who's bluffing does instinctively out of fear of being discovered.

Misinterpreting nervousness can be an extremely expensive poker mistake. That's why I want you to profit by understanding what makes a player shake, what makes him jittery and what makes him impatient.

When a player makes a very big hand, he may begin to shake noticeably. In general, this is a *release of tension* and should not be interpreted as concern over his fate. Many millions of dollars (and that's no exaggeration) are lost every year by calling players who suddenly begin to tremble.

Here's something even more important. If a player has a big hand, has already bet and is waiting for your call, he may tap his finger rhythmically on the table. He is usually unaware he's performing this impatient act. Among many players, even some world-class players, you'll see this (usually in a limit game) only when they are already pretty certain of winning the pot and the only remaining suspense is whether or not you'll call. If this is their habit and once in a while they bet but do *not* tap a finger, you can be almost 100 % sure they're either bluffing or they feel the hand is vulnerable.

Remember, most players show obvious outward nervousness *only* when they're in very little danger. If they're in great jeopardy, they struggle to control their nervousness until their fate is decided. Yes, they're nervous, but they won't let you know it if they can help it. One nervous clue to bluffing is very shallow breathing or even the holding of breath.

Additionally, players may be afraid to look at you *or* the pot. On the other hand, they may have read somewhere that players who won't look you in the eye are apt to be bluffing, so they'll compensate by staring at you blatantly. Make sure your opponent isn't trying to fool you, lest you make an erroneous conclusion about his behavior. If you're bound and determined to interpret eye contact, then the most common sign that an opponent is bluffing is if he'll look at you very briefly, offer a semi-smile and then glance away quickly. That's an attempt to look you in the eye and act unafraid. The action is cut short because the player can't maintain the act under great pressure. In that case, call.

Keep in mind that players who are bluffing genuinely bolster themselves and keep their movements reserved (except for any conscious acts they may try to convey). This means if a player has bet and his knee is jittering beneath the table (you can usually see, feel or sense this), then it is extremely unlikely that he's bluffing. If he normally jerks his knee up and down between and during hands, expect him to *stop* if ever he bluffs. This is a very important tell. Its *Value Per Hour* is much greater than most unaware tells, more than $3 in a typical $10 limit game.

There are other signs of nervousness and impatience that can't be seen. These are discussed under *Chapter 8— The Sounds of Tells*.

Let's look at two tells dealing with nervousness...

# TELL #10

**TITLE:**

It's exciting to come out fighting!

**CATEGORY:**

Nervousness.

**DESCRIPTION:**

In Photo 15, the player looks at his final seven-stud card. On the board he has three of clubs, eight of hearts, five of spades and six of hearts. You're probably wondering what his first two hole cards were, so I'll tell you: five of hearts, four of hearts. This means that as he looks at his river card (seventh card), he has a pair of fives, a possible straight, a possible flush *and* a possible straight flush.

In Photo 16 the magnitude of what he's caught is registering in his mind as he begins to tremble. You can tell, because his right hand is slightly blurry. By the time he completes his bet (Photo 17) his right hand is really shaking.

You guessed it, he made the straight flush! Also notice that his left hand continues to grip the river card. He's not looking at it anymore. He's merely pinching it hard in an effort to keep his left hand from shaking also. That's somewhat unusual. Often, a player in this situation would put the river card face down on the table and guard it.

**MOTIVATION:**

Made hand. No control.

## RELIABILITY:

Weak players = 99%
Average players = 95%
Strong players = 92%

## VALUE PER HOUR:

$1 limit = $1.50
$10 limit = $5.20
$100 limit = $49.50

## DISCUSSION:

The shaking is uncontrollable. Remember, it's a *release of tension,* not fear, that makes this player shake as he bets.

## BEST STRATEGY:

Pass, unless you also hold something thrilling.

---

### *Caro's Law of Tells #4*
*A trembling bet is a force to be feared.*

---

***Photo 15:***
*This player is looking at his final card in seven stud.*

***Photo 16:***
*He reaches for his chips, beginning to tremble slightly.*

***Photo 17:***
*Now he's shaking badly, while making his bet.*

## PLAY BY PLAY:

Be sure you're comfortable with the following chart before proceeding. You might wish to review *Chapter 3— Using MCU Poker Charts*.

Let's look a different example of how this tell works in a seven-card stud game. You're in seat #2.

## MCU Poker Chart

*Game:* Seven-card stud *Structure:* $10 ante, $15 low card forced bring-in bet, $50 bets on starting hand and 4th street, $100 thereafter.

| 1 | *2* | 3 | 4 | 5 | 6 | 7 | 8 | Pot |
|---|---|---|---|---|---|---|---|---|
| a10 | a10 | a10 | a10 | a10 | a10 | a10 | a10 | $80 |
| [down] | J♥J / A♠A | [down] | [down] | [down] | [down] | [down] | [down] | **Starting hands** <<< |
| 7♦7 | J♠J | 10♦10 | 2♦2 | K♣K | K♠K | 10♥10 | 4♥4 | |
| ▲50 | =50[1] | — | ▶b15 — | =15 =50◀ | — | — | — | $245 |
| 6♦6 | 4♣4 | | | J♦J | | | | **4th Street** <<< |
| =50 | =50[2]◀ | | | ▶ 50 | | | | $395 |
| 6♥6 | A♦A | | | 9♣9 | | | | **5th Street** <<< |
| ▶✔ =100 =200◀ | ✔[3] ▲200 | | | 100 =200 | | | | $995 |
| Q♣Q | 4♠4 | | | 7♣7 | | | | **6th Street** <<< |
| ▶✔ =100◀ | 100 | | | =100 | | | | $1,295 |
| [down] | 8♠8 | | | [down] | | | | **River** <<< |
| ▶100[4] ▲300 | —[5] | | | ▲200[6] =300◀ | | | | $1,895 |
| 4♦4 / 3♦3 / 5♦5 | J♥J / A♠A / 8♦8 | | | K♥K / A♣A / 2♣2 | | | | **Hole cards revealed (river card last)** <<< |
| WIN | | | | | | | | |

> **Chart key:** Action reads left to right, top to bottom. Each betting round begins ▶ with and ends with ◀ . Other markings and symbols: a (ante); b (blind bet); ✔ (check); = (call); ▲ (raise); – (fold); ● (dealer position, a.k.a. "the button"). A seat number surrounded by asterisks (for example, *1*) is your seat. Any wager not preceded by a symbol is a voluntary first bet. Wagers indicate the total invested on a betting round. The money in the rightmost column indicates total pot size after the betting.

## MCU POKER CHART NOTES
*(See corresponding numbers within chart.)*

**1)** There are only two opposing cards ranking higher than your jack—both of them kings. The first king makes a call of the forced $15 bring-in bet. This can mean anything from three clubs, to all high cards with straight possibilities, to just a single buried ace, to a small buried pair, to a pair of kings, to nothing much at all. Players call bring-in bets for all kinds of reasons. Hunches, spontaneous brain surges, you name it.

Now Player #1 "completes the bet" by raising to $50—the betting limit on this round. You call. If you're thinking about folding here, you're probably playing way too tight. Remember, it's just as bad to throw a hand away that has an expectation of profit than to play a hand that doesn't. In other words, you lose profit by not taking advantage of hands that are strong enough *and* you lose profit by playing hands that are not strong enough. With the king just calling, another king out of play, a raise from a door card seven, and no higher card left to threaten you, this hand clearly has a profit expectation. It isn't really a close decision, and if you think it is, you need to reevaluate how you're playing seven-card stud.

Anyway, the king calls and the pot is now $245.

**2)** On the next betting round, you catch a decidedly

unhelpful four. Player #5 bets with king-jack showing. That's kind of surprising, right? Maybe he had a pair of kings after all. It's not likely that he made a pair of jacks, because you hold two of them. Maybe he had queen-ten in the hole and now has an open-end straight draw. Maybe he's just leveraging his high cards, hoping to chase you and the other opponent out of the pot.

You're just never going to know these things for sure in the absence of tells. And anybody who says they can figure out exactly what opponents have at these early betting stages of stud, against typical players who often decide what to do at whim, is just telling you wrong. Player #1 calls without hesitation. You call.

**3)** The limits have now doubled from $50 to $100. Player #1 makes an exposed pair of sixes and checks. You should now consider betting. In fact, I bet most of the time in this situation. Player #5 caught a nine and might have made a straight, but that's not the most likely thing. He's more likely to have caught a fourth club or maybe he had a pair of kings all along. Maybe something else. You've just made aces-up, catching an ace, and when that happens to me, I don't want to let my opponents get another card for free. I'm probably best and I want them to pay the price. So, betting is my usual play. But you decide to check. And, you know what? That's not a bad idea, either.

In poker, you have to mix it up and keep your opponents off guard. Besides, Player #5 bet last round and he's an aggressive opponent, so he might bet this round, too. We give it a try. Sure enough, Player #5 wings out there with a $100 bet. Player #1 calls it. Now you could just call if you wanted, and that's what I'd do sometimes. If you just call, you're not tipping off Player #5 that you have anything. If he's bluffing or betting a weak hand, you'll probably prefer that he not change his mind on the next round. You might want to either check-call or check-raise on the next betting round, but if you check-raise right now, you might have identified your strength prematurely and won't be able to let your opponent tighten his own noose by continuing to bet next.

Of course, other thoughts are going through your head. You might not have the best hand, for instance. But Player #1 almost certainly doesn't have three sixes, so you feel safe that you have him trapped. He probably has a straight draw or a flush draw, you figure. Maybe sevens-up. Maybe something else. You decide to raise, which is probably what you had in mind when you checked. You get two calls. Fine.

**4)** After an uneventful sixth card, which saw Player #5 pick up another club for a not-too-likely—but possible—flush and your bet being called by both opponents, we move on to the final action at the river (last card, facedown). Your card doesn't help, and you still have aces-up (actually three pair, but the third one doesn't count).

Player #1 suddenly bets. The pot is awfully big and you're getting over 13-to-1 odds to call. Of course, it's not really that good, because Player #5 might now have you beat, even if your hand is stronger than the bettor's. Still, Player #1 often bluffs and sometimes pushes two pair for value, so this is a call you're normally going to make. You wouldn't expect to win most of the time, but you would expect to win enough of the time to show a nice profit. Nobody believes strongly that you have aces-up, because you have no pair showing. They may consider it a possibility, but it's not what they expect.

THE TELL. Player #1, who was previously in control, begins to tremble as he places the chips in the pot. You know what that means. We just talked about it. It *doesn't* mean that he's nervous about bluffing. Bluffers bolster themselves. This is a release of tension. The suspense is over. He's made a very big hand and this is simply nervous excitement. He can't control it. But, look! There's something else that doesn't even happen in the following photos. He's now gripping the edge of the table hard, trying to conceal his shaking. Why? He's embarrassed by it, so you can be sure the shaking wasn't an act. And, in fact, it almost never is—unless the player has read this book.

**5)** So, Player #1 made a big hand, pure and simple. You're not sure what it is. It could be anything from a big flush on up. Maybe a full house. Maybe four of a kind. It's big, though. Certainly it's bigger than aces-up, so you fold. Excellent!

**6)** But Player #5 doesn't know this tell. He's made a flush and raises. He gets reraised and calls. Maybe he should have called the initial bet on the strength of the ace-high flush, but he should never have raised. That mistake cost him an extra $200 this time. Player #1 had a straight flush— but we suspected that, didn't we?

# TELL #11

**TITLE:**

I can't believe I'm betting! Where can I hide?

**CATEGORY:**

Nervousness.

**DESCRIPTION:**

There are two things you should notice here. The bettor (left) is covering his mouth with his hand. That's the tell we're about to examine. But you should also observe that the player at right is reaching for his chips and staring at the bettor. This latter tell will be discussed in *Chapter 6— Tells From Actors.*

**MOTIVATION:**

There's a reasonable chance that the bettor is covering his mouth to make close scrutiny of his face difficult. He's unaware that he's doing it, though. The reason he unconsciously wants to avoid examination is that he's probably bluffing.

**RELIABILITY:**

Weak players = 71%
Average players = 62%
Strong players = 57%

**VALUE PER HOUR:**

$1 limit = $0.27
$10 limit = $0.54
$100 limit = $1.35

## DISCUSSION:

Those of you familiar with kinesics and "body language" may have already figured out why the bettor is probably bluffing. Many people who put their hands on or near their mouths are not telling the whole truth. Some people have developed this habit for self-conscious reasons even when telling the gospel truth, so this tell isn't 100% accurate, only a fairly good indicator.

A 1980 study of lowball players that I conducted in Gardena, California showed only moderate evidence in support of this tell. The scope of the study was 67 clear hand-near mouth instances. In 44 cases, the bettor was called, but won the pot only 12 times. Three times the bettor was raised and threw his hand away. Although that would seem to indicate that this tidbit can be used pretty effectively at the poker table, be cautious.

First, of 32 times that the bettor lost to the caller, we cannot assume that he (or she, as it sometimes happened) was always bluffing. On a few occasions, he may have thrown away a legitimate betting hand upon seeing a stronger hand shown by the caller. Second, it's mathematically possible that the bettor was *never* bluffing on the 20 occasions that he wasn't called.

Such a circumstance would dramatically alter the results of the study. In fact, I specifically noted one case where the bettor wasn't called and showed down a six-four, the second best possible hand, just because he was proud of it. Even considering those words of caution, hand-near-mouth players appeared to be either bluffing or holding weak hands most of the time. This is one of those popular body language behaviorisms which has been well publicized. Its poker value seems to be only marginal. Nevertheless, it's probable that players who position their hands near their mouths are more likely to be bluffing than those who don't.

## BEST STRATEGY:

When in doubt, call with marginal hands and even weak hands.

---

### Caro's Law of Tells #5
*In the absence of indications to the contrary, call any bettor whose hand covers his mouth*

---

*Photo 18:*
*The man at left is bluffing. Where is his left hand?*

# Double-Checking

Players double-check their hands for various reasons. If they've already bet and, under the threat of a call, they look back and *continue to stare* at the hand, there's a very high probability that they are weak or bluffing. That's an *act* designed to make you think they're studying a powerful hand. We'll handle that related subject in *Chapter 6—Tells From Actors.* It's also discussed in *Chapter 7—Some General Tells,* in Section XXII, titled *Gaining Information.* Right now we're dealing with something entirely different.

This section is about genuine instinctive double-checking. You can distinguish it from the *acted* double-check, because in the genuine kind the player will look only long enough to determine whatever he must. Then he'll usually look away and guard his hand. But in cases where that genuine second look finds a bad hand, the player might decide to keep staring at it (for reasons relating to acting). Whether or not the original motive for the double-check was genuine, if the player continues to stare he then holds a weak hand.

If he peeks quickly, then glances away, you must ask yourself: *What could this opponent be checking for?* Usually the answer is apparent. If it's seven stud through fifth street (the fifth card has been dealt) and all three exposed cards are suited, then a quick glance to his hole cards probably means the player is checking to see if he has one more card of that suit. That tell is important because you know immediately that he does not have *two* cards of that suit, so he doesn't yet have a flush. Had he held two suited cards, he'd know it immediately, since the fifth card would have given him the flush he was hoping for. If a player hits a third suited card, then looks quickly at his hole cards, you must reason he does not have a flush and you can confidently bet hands you would otherwise have checked.

Suppose you're playing draw lowball and, after a rash of raises, your opponent draws one card. Suppose, further, that he is guarding the four cards that he's keeping in one hand. With the other hand he reaches for the card he's just drawn and peeks at it. Then he immediately turns his attention to his other cards, double-checking briefly. This should tell you that he caught a *low* card and either made the strong hand or paired. You should, therefore, revise your normal strategy by not betting anything but a premium hand. You should definitely not bet a smooth eight (like 8-5-3-2-A), because your opponent either made a much better hand and will raise, or he paired and will not call. So, you must check. If he subsequently bets, you should call with your eight *only* if you would also call with a king. That's because your eight can win only if he paired and is bluffing. If an eight wins, a king would win also.

Remember, players double-check for a reason. It's your job to figure out what that reason is. Here are some pictures...

# TELL #12

## TITLE:
What was my *other* card?

## CATEGORY:
Double-check.

## DESCRIPTION:
In Photo 19, the man on the left took the initiative by betting. This is seven stud and his exposed card was a king. His opponent's card was a jack. In Photo 20, the man catches an eight offsuit to go with his king. Immediately (and only *briefly,* though not proven by the photo) he looks back at his hole cards.

## MOTIVATION:
He simply wants to check his hole cards to see if the eight helped him.

## RELIABILITY:
Weak players = 70 %
Average players = 65 %
Strong players = 52%

## VALUE PER HOUR:
$1 limit = $0.15
$10 limit = $1.20
$100 limit = $1.50

## DISCUSSION:
When this player catches the small card and double-checks, you can be pretty sure he has some other small card in the hole. That small card did not have

relevance until now. Why? Probably because he had a pair of kings to begin with and some secondary card that was not worth remembering. Catching the eight made him check to see if he caught two pair. If both his face-up cards were suited, a motive for a double-check could be to see if he has one more of that suit in the hole.

## BEST STRATEGY:

Figure that there's a better than average chance that this opponent has a pair of kings and a fair chance he has kings-up. There is almost no chance he has either three kings or three eights. And it's very unlikely that he has a high kicker to go with a pair of kings. Keep these factors in mind, consider your own hand and play accordingly.

*Photo 19:*
*It's seven stud. The man at center is betting on third street. His face-up card is a king. His opponent holds a jack.*

*Photo 20:*
*Now we advance to fourth street. The player at center catches an eight to go with his king, and now he double checks his cards.*

# TELL #13

## TITLE:
One of my cards was red?

## CATEGORY:
Double-check.

## DESCRIPTION:
In Photo 21, the player watches the flop. In Photo 22, he realizes that all three flop cards are diamonds and he begins to double-check his hold 'em hand.

## MOTIVATION:
He wants to find out if he has a diamond.

## RELIABILITY:
Weak players = 90%
Average players = 85 %
Strong players = 75 %

## VALUE PER HOUR:
$1 limit = $0.20
$10 limit = $3.00
$100 limit = $13.50

## DISCUSSION:
Players remember denominations (such as king, seven, deuce) more readily than they do suits. Only if both hole cards are suited, are unsophisticated hold 'em players apt to be certain of their *exact* cards before the flop. For this reason, if the flop is suited, players must look back to see if they have a card of that suit. When you see a player peek again at his hand, it should tell you that he does not already

have a complete flush. However, he may have one card of the suit flopped. His double-check should also let you know that he doesn't have two pair or trips because then he'd know it and he wouldn't need to look.

This latter conclusion is a bit dangerous with some players, since they may hold hands like king-seven of clubs, see the flop come king-queen seven of diamonds and need to check to see if the seven *also* paired them (they can usually remember that the king paired them). In any case, this tell lets us know almost for sure that our opponent doesn't have a flush. This is one reason why you should be watching your opponents when the flop is spread. You can always look at the board later; it won't change.

### BEST STRATEGY:

If you hold king-jack (top pair with second best possible kicker) and you would bet if the flop weren't suited, you should consider betting anyway against this opponent. If you hold king-queen (two big pair) in no limit and this opponent subsequently moves all in against you, you should be more willing to call than you usually would. That's because there's a good chance he holds something other than a flush.

Perhaps his hand is queen of clubs with ace of diamonds, giving him a draw to the best possible flush *and* a quality pair. Your exact decision in a no limit game would be based on many other factors. Remember, any weak-to-average player who double-checks after the flop is giving you important information to weigh while making your decision.

***Photo 21:***
*The player is watching the dealer spread
the flop in hold 'em.*

***Photo 22:***
*The flop is three diamond-suited cards. As soon as he
sees it, the player begins to look back at his hand.*

# Fearlessness

If I tell you that players who hold cinch winners are unafraid, you'll say: *So what? Everyone in the world knows that.* True. But not everyone knows how players act at the poker table when they're unafraid. For one thing, players who are fearless are more apt to engage in natural conversation. If someone's holding a royal flush, you can ask him to comment on the politics of the day and he'll be able to talk in a relaxed, rational manner. Had he been bluffing, he'd be apt to either remain silent or force some hazy conversation. What he'd say would be less rational than usual. Don't believe me? Try asking players questions after they've bet into big pots. The ones with the dynamite hands will talk freely; the ones with the vulnerable hands will either remain silent, force their speech or talk gibberish.

What else can I tell you about fearless players who are holding winning hands? Well, it turns out that they sometimes smile broadly. Hey, you've hung around this world for a number of years. You know as well as I do how to tell the difference between a forced smile and a broad genuine smile. When you see a genuine smile, figure the player is happy about his hand. When you see a player force a smile after betting, there's a good chance he's bluffing.

Similarly, any player who has a giggling fit is almost certainly not bluffing (except in a very small game where his fate doesn't matter to him). A genuine giggle is hard to fake. Also, players have no motive to fake a giggle because, strangely enough, giggles don't make their opponents pass; giggles bring attention and make opponents suspicious.

Remember what we talked about in Section IV on *Nervousness.* People who bet and continue to move about impatiently are apt to have big hands. Players who are bluffing don't want to do anything that might trigger your call. Many bluffers feel instinctively that they must remain almost unmoving for fear of giving their hand away and getting called. That's why when you see a very animated player who has bet, you should figure he has a good hand. There is an exception: Some players will use motions and comments specifically designed to make you throw your hand away. When players *act* like they hold big hands, they deserve your call because they're usually weak. But when they're just being themselves, making movements and not trying to restrain themselves, it's unlikely that they're bluffing or even worried.

There is one peculiar habit displayed by some players who are unafraid. These are usually friendly players who after betting may make some gruff remark. Maybe you came right out and asked if he was bluffing and he replied, "Just play the game." You thought this kind of unfriendly remark was out of character for him. What should you do? Probably pass. Players who are bluffing are generally afraid to engage in hostilities. They don't want to make you call out of anger. Ask a bluffer if he's bluffing and you're more apt to hear him chirp something like, "Let me check and see," coupled with a forced smile, or simply "Yes," said in a deliberately unconvincing manner.

---

### *Caro's Law of Tells #6*
*A genuine smile usually means a genuine hand;*
*a forced smile is a bluff.*

---

### *Caro's Law of Tells #7*
*The friendlier a bettor is,*
*the more apt he is to be bluffing.*

---

Considering Laws #6 and #7, keep in mind that most players can smile genuinely only when they're feeling fearless. And players are without fear because they hold probable winning hands. The reason bluffers are apt to be friendly is that they are afraid to seem intimidating. They are acting nice so you won't call. Conversely, some players may try to intimidate you into calling when they have winning hands by acting gruffer than their usual manner.

Got it? Great! Now here's a photographic tell that deals with cigarettes...

# TELL #14

## TITLE:
Victory and the taste of tobacco.

## CATEGORY:
Fearlessness.

## DESCRIPTION:
After placing his bet, the man in the suit grasps his cigarette and takes a big puff (Photo 23). In Photo 24 we see him awaiting the call and exhaling noticeably.

## MOTIVATION:
No fears. Impatience.

## RELIABILITY:
Weak players = 60%
Average players = 60%
Strong players = 60%

## VALUE PER HOUR:
$1 limit = $0.15
$10 limit = $1.20
$100 limit = $7.50

## DISCUSSION:
Players who are bluffing and are therefore afraid will be reluctant to exhale their cigarette smoke in a conspicuous manner. Remember, bluffers try to do nothing to bring attention to themselves and promote a call. Most bluffers would like to be invisible if they could. When a player exhales a huge cloud of smoke, he's not as likely to be afraid of your call. This is an "unaware" tell that's just about

equally valid for strong players as for weak players. It will occur more times per hour, however, in smaller games. Since this tell is only 60% reliable, keep in mind that the opposite of what you expect will frequently happen. Occasionally you'll see a cloud of smoke accompany a bluff, even though your clue should weigh in the opposite direction.

## BEST STRATEGY:

When you are in doubt, pass.

*Photo 23:*
*The man in the suit has made his bet and now he takes a drag from his cigarette.*

*Photo 24:*
*He exhales a cloud of cigarette smoke.*

# Glancing at Chips

This is the most valuable clue you're likely to uncover among those who are unaware of their behavior.

Take beginning players, for instance; they do it. Even average players do it. You'll see this tell when you're watching players with years and years of poker experience. But that's not the best part. World-class pros exhibit this tell! What more could you ask for? Well, there is more. Many *world champions* provide you with this tell regularly (or at least they used to—until this book came out).

The principle is simple, so let's make it a Law. . .

> ***Caro's Law of Tells #8***
> *A player glances secretly at his chips only when he's considering a bet—and almost always because he's helped his hand.*

You must determine, first, that the glance is not an act. If players stare for a long time at their chips *while they think you're watching* that's probably an act—but you won't see it happen often. Usually, they'll look at their hand (or the flop or the stud card they just caught), then immediately to their chips for a brief moment, then away. That's practically never an act because they don't figure you're watching them right then.

Michael Wiesenberg, noted poker and computer authority, contributes a related tell. Players may glance at *your* chips when they intend to bet. This is much less common than glancing at their own chips. Often it means the same thing (that the player likes his hand and is preparing to wager), especially if the glance is immediate and fleeting. However, be advised that, if your opponent looks at your chips long after he realizes what his cards are, he might be measuring whether he can get away with a bluff. He needs to know what your stack looks like before assessing his bluffing possibilities. For that reason, it's more difficult to interpret the tell when your opponent looks at your chips instead of his own. Also, keep in mind that in no-limit games, players may ostentatiously stare at your chips before bluffing. In order for the glance at *your* chips to reliably mean that the player has a good hand and intends to bet, that glance must *be* brief and the player must be *unaware* that you're watching.

For the most part, expect the player to glance at his own chips. We shall dwell on this a little longer, because it's so important.

If you want to use this tell, you must follow this advice:

• When the cards are dealt, don't look at them; watch your opponent!

• When the flop lands in hold 'em, don't look at it; watch your opponent!

• When the next card arrives in stud, don't look at it; watch your opponent!

# TELL #15

## TITLE:

Love card, lots of chips, look yonder.

## CATEGORY:

Glancing at Chips.

## DESCRIPTION:

Here is a good example of a very important tell. In some games, average players could be big winners if they did nothing but look for this tell and play their normal game. First, the player sees his new seven-stud card. Good catch! At this moment his mind tingles gleefully. Automatically, his eyes fall to his chips. Sometimes he may lower his head briefly, which makes detection easier. That's what's happening here. More often, his head will move only slightly and his *eyes* will find his chips. In that case, you must look more closely. In the last photo, the player is looking away and pretending to be unimpressed by his last card. This is a *Weak Means Strong* indication which will be covered in *Chapter 6—Tells From Actors*.

## MOTIVATION:

The glance at the chips is instinctive.

## RELIABILITY:

Weak players = 98 %
Average players = 96%
Strong players = 90%

## VALUE PER HOUR:
$1 limit = $2.60
$10 limit = $8.00
$100 limit = $41.00

## DISCUSSION:
Players will glance only quickly at their chips, then away. You must be looking at the exact moment it happens. It is a very big mistake not to be watching your seven stud opponents when the new cards arrive. You can always look at your own card later. A quick glance at their chips means they helped their hand.

## BEST STRATEGY:
Look for sandbagging (checking and then raising) opportunities. Sandbagging can be a powerful poker weapon, but it's even more desirable if you know almost for sure that your opponent will bet, as you do in this tell. If you don't have a strong hand, don't hope to catch this man bluffing. He won't be. And, certainly, don't try to bluff him.

*Photo 25:*
*It's seven stud and an ace is being*
*dealt to the man at center.*

***Photo 26:***
*He immediately glances down at his chips.*

***Photo 27:***
*Now he looks away as if uninterested.*

# TELL #16

**TITLE:**

Great flop, better make sure my chips are still here.

**CATEGORY:**

Glancing at Chips.

**DESCRIPTION:**

The quick-glance-at-chips tell occurs very frequently in hold 'em. In Photo 28, the flop registers in the player's mind. Instinctively she looks at her chips (Photo 29). But you have to watch closely or you'll miss it, because by Photo 30—less than one second later— she's looking toward the flop.

**MOTIVATION:**

An instinctive reaction after the flop helps her hand.

**RELIABILITY:**

Weak players = 98 %
Average players = 96%
Strong players = 90%

**VALUE PER HOUR:**

$1 limit = $2.75
$10 limit = $9.50
$100 limit = $40.00

**DISCUSSION:**

This is very similar to—and, in fact, conceptually identical to—the previous tell. This woman does not look away from the action, however. Instead, she pretends to study the flop. Of course, she already knows very well that the flop helped her, so she doesn't need to study. She's just trying to make you think she's weaker than she is. If you were watching the flop—as even most professional players invariably do—you would have missed this very profitable opportunity and you wouldn't know that the woman now holds a strong hand.

## BEST STRATEGY:

You need a stronger hand than usual to compete. Don't bluff this woman. Don't expect to catch her bluffing. If you have a mind to check and raise, this is a good opportunity.

*Photo 28:*
*It's hold 'em, and here comes the flop.*

***Photo 29:***
*Immediately the player looks at her chips.*

***Photo 30:***
*But the glance is brief and now she is
pretending to study the flop.*

# Sudden Interest

Always be alert for a player who suddenly perks up and plays a pot. Usually it takes a genuine hand to rouse a player from a lethargic condition and get him interested in gambling. Often a player will be daydreaming or leaning back, content to wait for the good hands (usually because he's winning). Look! Suddenly, he leans forward and adjusts his posture. He may merely squirm on his chair until he's sitting slightly straighter. This kind of mannerism means the player has a decent hand and is preparing to play.

Also, if he's humming or whistling (handled under *Chapter 8—The Sounds of Tells)* and then mysteriously stops, it's very likely he holds a hand that pleases him. Normally players who are involved in conversation and then fall silent or lose their ability to form meaningful sentences are about to play a hand.

Those are some signs of sudden interest.

Look at Photo 9 in Section I, *Noncombat Tells*. That man is leaning back, relaxing. He is not likely to play the next pot. Contrast that posture to the following...

# TELL #17

**TITLE:**
This hand might be worth the bother.

**CATEGORY:**
Sudden Interest.

**DESCRIPTION:**
This player has been sitting back with his arms folded, watching the world go by. He's winning and doesn't want to risk much of his profit. Suddenly, he receives a jack for his face-up card in seven stud. Extending his arm, and still leaning back, he looks at his hole cards. Then, suddenly, he begins to adjust his posture, shuffling until he is sitting straighter and leaning somewhat forward.

**MOTIVATION:**
He is unconsciously preparing to get involved.

**RELIABILITY:**
Weak players = 77%
Average players = 65%
Strong players = 55%

**VALUE PER HOUR:**
$1 limit = $0.15
$10 limit = $0.33
$100 limit = $0.75

**DISCUSSION:**
It's a mistake to think a player who suddenly adjusts his posture is acting in a manner he hopes will mislead you. Much more frequently, the player is unaware of his

action, particularly if he's a novice. You can substantiate this by noting the times when players adjust their postures; you'll discover that it's usually when they are not conscious that you're watching them, making it unlikely that they're acting. Furthermore, the adjustment will usually be brief— also indicating the player isn't trying to draw attention to himself. The exact strength of this seven-stud player's hand depends somewhat on the cards of his opponents, his position relative to the first bettor and how heavy the action is so far. What we do know is that he likes his cards.

## BEST STRATEGY:

Unless this man holds a strong speculative hand, such as king, queen, jack of the same suit, he probably has at least a pair of jacks. It's likely that he has a buried pair even higher than jacks or even three of a kind. So plan your tactics accordingly, enter the pot with caution and don't try to bluff.

*Photo 31:*
*This man is adjusting his posture and sitting straighter than before.*

# Tough Decisions

One strange thing about *limit* poker players—beginners and great ones, too—is that they don't mind letting you know when they have a tough decision.

However, the same is *not* true of no-limit players. In *limit* games, there's a common trait among players who have been bet into and are now faced with a dilemma. They may grumble, discuss the hand aloud, or even sigh and say something like, "Oh, golly, I wish you wouldn't have bet. Now what should I do?" Very often, they'll rock back in their chairs and contemplate.

There's one truth you should always keep in mind. Although players are invariably actors on occasions, they seldom waste a lot of your time and theirs in a limit game if there's no *real* decision involved. Don't expect a player to use thirty seconds to consider a call, then raise. That sort of maneuver is unwelcome in limit games and few players risk their popularity by using it. (Novices sometimes do it, not realizing it's rude.) The reason players don't spend a lot of time *acting* like they're unsure and then raising in limit poker is quite simple. The amount of money at stake relative to the size of the pot is seldom overwhelming. In a no-limit game, there may be a total of $500 already bet and a player now wagers another $500. Here the opponent starts to ponder. There's a good chance that he's putting on an act and will end up raising.

If he decides to add $5,000 to the pot, the original bettor might also decide to take a long time before making his decision. That's the way of no-limit poker; hesitation is reasonable.

But, let's say you're playing $20 straight limit (where every bet must be exactly $20). There's $100 in the pot already and now someone bets $20. In response, a player grumbles, leans back and starts to wonder. This is a sign of a genuine dilemma. He's probably considering whether or not to call; raising is not among his options. Remember, the pace in a limit game is much faster than the pace in a no-limit game. Also, decisions in limit games are usually proportionally less important. Keeping those two things in mind, it's easy to see why long hesitation in a limit game usually means a genuine tough decision.

So what should you do if an opponent is showing signs of not knowing whether or not to call?

First, let's examine why a player might be in doubt. Obviously, most rational opponents are in doubt because they don't know if a call is a good investment. In-depth mathematics is not the focus of this book; however, if a pot is $80 and a call would cost $10, the player must decide if he has at least one chance in nine of winning. If he figures to win more than one such pot out of nine, he's making a good investment—take my word for it. A hesitant player probably feels he has *almost exactly* one chance in nine of winning, even if his evaluation is merely unconscious or intuitive. Your strategy is simple. If you made a legitimate bet with any meaningful hand, you probably want his call. If you're bluffing, you don't.

Remember that, against typical opponents, almost all your physical actions will encourage a call. Players came to the game wanting to put their money in action. If you have the best hand, you should provide your opponent with excuses for making losing calls. Shuffle your cards, talk gibberish, smile insanely, tap the table. All these things bring attention to yourself, make your opponent suspicious, and give him an excuse to call.

So, now you know the following: (1) When an opponent in a limit poker game hesitates for a long time or gives any other indication that he is bothered by your bet, he is probably sincerely uncertain about whether to call; (2) If you've bet with a strong hand, you should be animated and try to coax the opponent into calling; and (3) If you've bet with a weak hand, you should remain fairly still and, thus, encourage your opponent to pass.

It's important to note that most opponents will also remain still when bluffing and be more animated and friendly when holding a big hand. Even though you can use that knowledge against them, don't worry about providing these same tells yourself. It's very unlikely that your opponents are alert enough to read you correctly, so there's more profit to be won by using blatant manipulation than by wearing a poker face.

Now let's look at some genuine indecision...

# TELL #18

**TITLE:**

Let me think awhile.

**CATEGORY:**

Tough Decisions.

**DESCRIPTION:**

All seven cards have been dealt out in this stud game. The player at left has been doing the betting most of the way. But on the final card, the woman does the betting (Photo 32). At this point the man is faced with a genuine dilemma and must reevaluate his hand. He leans back to think it over (Photo 33).

**MOTIVATION:**

Genuine doubt.

**RELIABILITY:**

Weak players = 65 %
Average players = 70%
Strong players = 70%

**VALUE PER HOUR:**

$1 limit = $0.18
$10 limit = $1.20
$100 limit = $6.30

**DISCUSSION:**

Players seldomly delay limit poker games by taking extra time to make a decision. When this man leans back and considers his situation, it's probably a genuine borderline situation.

## BEST STRATEGY:

If you're the bettor faced with this reaction, you should encourage the call if you've made the bet on the strength of your hand. If you're bluffing, discourage the call. It's at times like this—when your opponent is experiencing genuine doubt—that manipulation works best. Also, if your opponent comes out raising after a long hesitation, there's almost a fifty percent chance that he's bluffing, and a call is correct.

*Photo 32:*
*The woman is betting her seven stud*
*hand into the man on the left.*

*Photo 33:*
*In response, he leans back and ponders.*

# Instant Reaction

Before trying a bluff, most players will take time to consider. In limit games, the delay may be only a few seconds, but *there is a delay*. A player needs time to calculate his chances and bolster his courage before bluffing. Additionally, bluffers are afraid to do anything unusual which might encourage your call. Even if it isn't on a conscious level, they know to not bluff too quickly. Experience has taught most players that an instantaneous bet looks suspicious and is not likely to succeed as a bluff.

For this reason, when a player draws three cards, looks at them, then glances *instantly* at his chips and begins to bet without hesitation, you can be pretty sure he has made a hand so obviously strong that it doesn't require consideration.

Conversely, if he checks instantly you can bet that it didn't help. Improvement, when followed by a check, requires evaluation—and evaluation takes time. True, a player might sometimes bet instantly in that smooth chain reaction that goes: look-at-cards, look-at-chips, grab-chips. Just remember, that happens only if the hand made is especially strong and no decision is required. Seldom will you see a player make aces-up and bet instantly. That's because betting aces-up in draw poker is usually a borderline decision that requires time for consideration. The same law governs all forms of poker.

***Caro's Law of Tells #9***
*If a player looks and then checks instantly,*
*it's unlikely that he improved his hand.*

***Caro's Law of Tells #10***
*If a player looks and then bets instantly,*
*it's unlikely that he's bluffing.*

# TELL #19

**TITLE:**

No help, I'll wait.

**CATEGORY:**

Instant Reaction.

**DESCRIPTION:**

This is draw poker and the player at center is drawing three to a pair of aces (Photo 34). In Photo 35, he looks and—almost at the same time—pounds his fist on the table to check.

**MOTIVATION:**

No reason to hesitate.

**RELIABILITY:**

Weak players = 94%
Average players = 87 %
Strong players = 60%

**VALUE PER HOUR:**

$1 limit = $0.45
$10 limit = $3.00
$100 limit = $7.50

**DISCUSSION:**

If this man had made aces-up or three aces, he'd have to evaluate the hand in the light of this new strength. This typically takes a few seconds. When this hesitation is not present, it's clear that the player didn't improve.

## BEST STRATEGY:

If you have any two pair or a stronger hand, bet. You'll even profit by betting a pair of aces with a king kicker.

*Photo 34:*
*The draw poker player (center) is asking for three cards.*

*Photo 35:*
*He looks and checks almost simultaneously.*

# TELL #20

## TITLE:
I probably don't need any help.

## CATEGORY:
Instant Reaction.

## DESCRIPTION:
It's draw poker, and the man wearing the hat doesn't announce his draw until after the opener (second from left) has declared that he needs three cards (Photo 36). In response, the hatted man draws one in Photo 37. In Photo 38, he looks at the card he's just drawn. This happens *before* the opener announces his bet or check.

## MOTIVATION:
The one-card draw is not suspenseful enough to delay looking.

## RELIABILITY:
Weak players = 62 %
Average players = 58%
Strong players = 55%

## VALUE PER HOUR:
$1 limit = $0.54
$10 limit = $2.40
$100 limit = $11.70

## DISCUSSION:
Here is another type of instant reaction. It's draw poker. When the opener takes three cards, the man in the hat realizes that two pair is the probable winner. So, if he has

two pair, he knows immediately that he has the better hand before the draw. He tells himself that although he may make a full house, he probably won't *need* to make one. In such a situation, the degree of suspense is less than maximum and the player is likely to look at his card as soon as he receives it. If, however, he is drawing one card to a straight or a flush, he must help his hand in order to win. He is then the underdog.

There is a great deal more suspense involved under such circumstances. In suspenseful all-or-nothing situations, many players enjoy not looking until they must. Therefore, when this player looks at his one-card draw instantly, you can figure it's likely that he has a two pair, not a straight or a flush attempt.

This tell is not nearly 100%, as you can see, but it works very consistently with some players. Among opponents who will sometimes look at their card immediately and sometimes wait, it's overwhelming that they hold two pair (or even three of a kind with a kicker) when they look instantly. This is *not* purely a draw poker tell. In all forms of poker, you can figure that players who won't look until they *must* are likely to need improvement.

### BEST STRATEGY:

If you are the opener who drew three cards, bet if you make aces-up or queens-up. You're likely to get a call from a smaller two pair—two pair which your opponent almost certainly won't bet for you if you check.

*Photo 36:*
*The player second from left is drawing three cards, while his opponent at center watches.*

*Photo 37:*
*The man at center draws one...*

*Photo 38:*
*...and then he looks at it immediately.*

# TELL #21

**TITLE:**
You go first.

**CATEGORY:**
Instant Reaction (opposite).

**DESCRIPTION:**
This sequence shows the opposite of what happened in the previous one. Instead of looking instantly at his one-card draw, the player at center decides to wait and heighten the suspense.

**MOTIVATION:**
He holds a suspenseful hand whose all-or-nothing fate need not be decided yet.

**RELIABILITY:**
Weak players = 62 %
Average players = 56%
Strong players = 54%

**VALUE PER HOUR:**
$1 limit = $0.60
$10 limit = $2.85
$100 limit = $12.00

**DISCUSSION:**
No matter what kind of poker game you're involved in, when you can determine which players need to improve their hand and which players already have a decent hand, you can confidently make bets when you would otherwise have checked, and you can check dangerous hands you

might otherwise have bet. See Tell #20 and remember that players who must improve to win are in more suspenseful situations than those who feel they might already have a winning hand. That's important, because players in suspenseful situations are likely to wait before looking; players in low pressure situations are apt to look right away.

## BEST STRATEGY:

Check all medium-strength hands.

***Photo 39:***
*The opener (player second from left) draws three.*

***Photo 40:***
*The man in the hat takes only one.*

***Photo 41:***
*The opener watches as the one-card
drawer refuses to look until later.*

***Photo 42:***
*Now the one-card drawer guards his hand
and waits for the opener to act.*

# Protecting a Hand

Most players unconsciously guard good cards more carefully than bad cards. While this is more common among weak players, the trait is found at all levels of play and in all forms of poker.

Even the rarely played five card stud provides instances of this tell, because players with good hands tend to show more concern when you reach toward their hole card. Of course, you must not actually touch or even physically approach the opponent's hole card—that's poor poker etiquette. But you can make an ambiguous gesture that your opponent might misinterpret as an invasion of his space. In response, an opponent holding a strong hand will usually jerk unconsciously and assume a more rigid position. He may even fend you off with a stiff arm used as a barrier. Players with weak hands are more lax. They wouldn't care if you reached all the way over and exposed the hole card. Then they could argue that they were entitled to a portion of the pot.

This kind of protective reaction applies to all varieties of poker. However, you don't need to make threatening gestures toward an opponent's cards to utilize this tell. Most opponents will give you clues without any provocation, and this is especially easy to understand if we focus on draw poker.

# TELL #22

**TITLE:**

I better not let these get away.

**CATEGORY:**

Protecting a Hand.

**DESCRIPTION:**

Most draw players look at their cards in a more clandestine manner than what's shown in Photo 43. In small-limit home games and in public casinos where flexible plastic cards are used, the method pictured is sometimes observed. In any case, what's important is whether the player protects his cards *after* he sees them. Two aces and a king on the first three cards is a nice catch, so in Photo 44, the player pushes them securely into his left hand. In Photo 45, the final two cards are viewed: ace and king. That gives this player aces-full. Photo 46 shows him squeezing this treasure very tightly between his fingers.

**MOTIVATION:**

Most people guard important belongings.

**RELIABILITY:**

Weak players = 90%
Average players = 80%
Strong players = 70%

**VALUE PER HOUR:**

$1 limit = $1.10
$10 limit = $4.40
$100 limit = $16.00

## DISCUSSION:

Be cautious in using this tell, because some players guard all hands. A few will even use a carefully guarded hand as a ploy to make you think that their weak hand is awesome. That's rare, though, because most players realize that the manner in which a hand is guarded is not something most opponents observe. Knowing this, a player who's weak will not generally go to the trouble of guarding his hand for deception. For that reason, protecting a hand is a topic that fits neatly into this chapter.

The governing truth is that closely protected hands are usually strong. Sometimes, you can even draw a correlation between the amount of protection and the exact strength of the hand. In this photo sequence, the player picks up a full house and makes certain it is secure. There's one other tell at work here, but it belongs in *Chapter 6—Tells From Actors*. It is this: In the final photo (46), the player is acting almost as if he's about to throw his hand away out of turn. That almost always means he has a good hand, as we'll soon see.

Speaking of acting, we'll also soon learn how the typical player might behave if he had been dealt garbage cards instead of a full house. Rather than guard them, he'd be likely to *stare* at them. But that's a topic we must deal with in the pages ahead, as we shift from players who are unaware to actors who are trying to deceive you.

## BEST STRATEGY:

Assume you're sitting two seats to the right of this player. You wouldn't have seen that he has aces-full, but you'd know he holds something pretty good. You should elect not to open the pot with marginal hands. If this player opens, you should pass with all borderline hands. If you hold an extremely strong hand yourself (say, a straight flush) in jacks-or-better-to-open, you might elect to check rather than open, knowing this player will open for you.

***Photo 43:***
*It's draw poker and, while the deal is in progress, the player looks at his first three cards.*

***Photo 44:***
*He shelters them in his left hand.*

***Photo 45:***
*He looks at his next two cards, which complete a full house.*

***Photo 46:***
*Immediately, he guards these also.*

# TELLS FROM ACTORS

In 1977, I contributed these words to Doyle Brunson's classic book *Super/System—A Course In Power Poker.*

"Most people are prevented from living the life they want. In childhood, they're required to do chores they hate. They grow up having to conform at school. As adults they must shake hands they don't want to shake, socialize with people they dislike, pretend they're feeling "fine" when they're feeling miserable, and *act* in control of situations where, in truth, they feel frightened and unsure.

These people—the majority of folks you meet every day—are actors. They present themselves to you as people different than they really are.

Deep within themselves they know they are not the same people they pretend to be. On an unconscious level, they think, "Hey, I'm so phony that if I don't act to disguise my poker hand, everyone will see right through me!"

And that's why the majority of these pitiful people are going to *give you* their money by always acting weak when they're strong and strong when they're weak."

There are six sections in this chapter in addition to the two titled *Weak Means Strong* and *Strong Means Weak.* But don't let that fool you. All of the tells discussed here in are related to those first two sections. Once you understand the basic concept and apply it, poker domination will become easy and your wallet will begin to bulge.

Before you can use the tells provided by an actor, you must be fairly certain that he's acting and not simply unaware. Determining that truth is not usually difficult. It's probably an act if the player has reason to believe you might be observing a specific mannerism *and* it is of obvious value to him that your conclusion is wrong. I'll say that again, so you don't simply rush past this powerful truth. An opponent is probably acting if: (1) He believes you're watching or listening; and (2) Your decision matters to him.

Since usually both those conditions must be true for a player to act, you may occasionally see beginners start to pass out of turn when they're genuinely not interested in the pot. They may be aware you're watching (the first condition), but your decision doesn't matter (the second condition) because they plan on passing anyway. Such straightforward tells are not usually the case, as we'll soon see. Most players feel an obligation to the game and, in this example, usually won't pass out of turn. Therefore, when they act as if to pass and are aware you're watching, there's a strong probability that they'll actually bet or raise.

Since a minority of players will not fall into the *weak means strong* and *strong means weak* mode, you should mentally note who they are so you won't err by perpetually applying these tells in those special cases.

Also keep in mind that, overall, strong players are less apt to provide you with tells than weak or average players. Beyond just denying you some of the more common tells, world-class opponents often try to deceive you by reversing some of the more obvious tells. That's right, they may sometimes act weak and *be* weak. You should place such opponents on a "tricky" list in your head and evaluate their behavior carefully.

Fortunately, even poker superstars will provide you with important tells quite regularly. But, for the most part, ordinary players are more predictable and more profitable.

# Weak Means Strong

Poker players like to fool you. If they can convince you that they have a weak hand when they have a strong hand, they figure they'll win a few extra calls and make a few extra dollars.

That reasoning is exactly right. If you let these actors succeed in fooling you, they'll win your money when they hold strong hands. Don't let that happen. The very same acts, which are designed to steal your money, will supply you with powerful information that can place your opponents' bankrolls at your mercy.

When players go out of their way to act weak, it's because they hold strong hands. Remember that. Would you expect a player who truly holds a weak hand to tell you he's in bad shape? That would be stupid. Would you expect a bluffer to tell you he's bluffing? Not me! If they act weak, it can only be because they're strong.

---

*Caro's Law of Tells #11*
*Disappoint any player who,*
*by acting weak, is seeking your call.*

---

# TELL #23

**TITLE:**

Ah, what's the difference? I bet.

**CATEGORY:**

Weak Means Strong.

**DESCRIPTION:**

Here's a seven-stud player who's accompanying his bet with a shrug.

**MOTIVATION:**

He wants to make you think he's unsure of his bet.

**RELIABILITY:**

Weak players = 93%

Average players = 90%

Strong players = 80%

**VALUE PER HOUR:**

$1 limit = $0.55

$10 limit = $3.20

$100 limit = $11.00

**DISCUSSION:**

Hey, what can I tell you about a shrug that you don't already know? If you ask a friend how he's feeling and you get a polite shrug in response, that's supposed to substitute for, "I'm not really sure. Things could be better." And that's exactly what a poker player is trying to convey when he shrugs and bets. He's suggesting he's not certain about the bet and that his hand could be a lot stronger. Well, don't you believe it! There's only one reason this guy would go out of his way to make you think he has a doubtful betting hand. It's because he holds an almost certain winner.

## BEST STRATEGY:

Call only with powerful hands; in fact, *just* call with most hands that suggest a raise. Don't try to bluff.

*Photo 47:*
*The man at center is shrugging.*

## PLAY BY PLAY:

The photo uses seven-card stud as an example game. This MCU Poker Chart deals with hold 'em. Most of the tells in this book don't relate to a single game. You'll see them almost everywhere you play. You're in seat #1.

**MCU Poker Chart**

*Game:* Hold 'em  *Structure:* $25 and $50 blinds, $50 bets on starting hand and flop, $100 thereafter.

| *1* | 2 | 3 | 4 | 5 | 6 | 7 | 8 | 9 | 10 | Pot |
|---|---|---|---|---|---|---|---|---|---|---|
| b25 | b50 | | | | | | | | ● | $75 |
| 10♦ / 9♦ | | | | | | | | | | **Starting hands** <<< |
| =100¹ =150⁴ | ▲150² | ▶50 — | — | — | =50 =150 | — | — | — | ▲100 =150 | $650 |
| | | | | | | | | | | **Flop** Q♦ Q♠ 9♠ |
| ▶✔⁴ — | ✔ =50◀ | | | | 50 | | | | =50 | <<< $800 |
| | | | | | | | | | | **Turn** 7♥ |
| | ▶✔ — | | | | ✔ ▲200 | | | | 100 =200◀ | <<< $1,200 |
| | | | | | | | | | | **River** 7♦ |
| | | | | | ▶100 | | | | =100◀ | <<< $1,400 |
| | | | | | A♥A Q♥Q WIN | | | | J♦J J♣J | **Two-card hands revealed** <<< |

**Chart key:** Action reads left to right, top to bottom. Each betting round begins ▶ with and ends with ◀. Other markings and symbols: a (ante); b (blind bet); ✔ (check); = (call); ▲ (raise); – (fold); ● (dealer position, a.k.a. "the button"). A seat number surrounded by asterisks (for example, *1*) is your seat. Any wager not preceded by a symbol is a voluntary first bet. Wagers indicate the total invested on a betting round. The money in the rightmost column indicates total pot size after the betting.

## MCU POKER CHART NOTES
*(See corresponding numbers within chart.)*

**1)** You're in the small blind. Your ten-nine suited is a hand you might sometimes throw away. But here it's probably profitable. You have bad position, because you'll have to act first on all subsequent rounds of betting, but the fact that the first player to act may have indicated weakness when he didn't raise the big blind (only called) is comforting. And the important fact that you're getting a 25 percent discount, because you only have to put in $75, not $100, to call the $100 bet is almost certainly enough to make this hand playable. Don't look for a big average profit when you play hands like this in the small blind, but you should earn *some* profit overall.

**2)** The big blind has an opportunity to just call, to fold, or to raise. Note that just calling here, with the intention of seeing the flop for free, is not as safe as it seems.

That's because his call won't *close the betting.* I use the term *close the betting* to mean that if a player calls, nobody else can raise afterward. This would have been the case had Player #3 raised and—acting before your call—both Player #6 and #10 called. As it is now, his call won't close the betting and, in fact, there are a whole lot of betting sequences that could work against Player #2 if he has a borderline hand—sequences that include more than one additional raise. But, in this case, Player #2 isn't worried about that, because he does the reraising himself. We'll never find out what he has, because he'll fold on the turn (4th board card).

**3)** When the action returns to you, this is an automatic call. There's already $600 out there and it costs you just $50 to call. You'll probably need to see a lucky flop, but you can't fold with these 12-to-1 pot odds. And, remember the concept we just talked about. This is a safe call, because it *will* close the betting.

**4)** You don't look at the flop, in accordance with other advice in this book. That's because you want to be spotting tells, and you can often do that by watching other players look at the flop. Nothing here, though. You are first to act. You seriously consider betting.

Because these are aggressive opponents, there's a chance that everyone played high cards without a queen, or pairs smaller than the nines you've just flopped—or something else entirely. If that's the case, you might be able to take the pot right now, benefit from calls, or just chase some potential winners out of the pot. All that can be good. But you'd be more likely to make that daring bet against one or two opponents. Three makes it more problematic. You decide to check. This is what I'd do most of the time, although I would frequently bet. Player #2 also checks. Player #6 bets $50. "Who didn't know that was coming?" you think to yourself, because Player #6 is one of the most consistent bluffers you've ever seen. He fires chips at every opportunity, with seeming disregard for what he's holding.

THE TELL. But, wait! He didn't just bet $50, he did something else at the same time—something you noticed. He semi-shrugged as he bet. It wasn't the blatant sort of shrug you see in the accompanying photo, but it was enough to get the message across. This player is trying to convey doubt about his hand, but he has none. It's an act. He has a queen! Almost nothing else would cause this reaction. He stopped raising before the flop, so it's unlikely he has a pocket pair of kings or aces, which would also make him proud. Sure, you're getting 15-to-1 pot odds to call, but that's not going to do you much good if your opponent holds a queen. And this classic tell makes it overwhelmingly likely that he does, so you fold. And, as you can see, you did the right thing.

# TELL #24

## TITLE:

Maybe I'll throw this card away, or maybe I'll raise. . .

## CATEGORY:

Weak Means Strong.

## DESCRIPTION:

It's seven stud and the player at left is betting his ten into his opponent's king. In response, the opponent suggests that he's going to pass by beginning to turn the king face down.

## MOTIVATION:

The opponent wants to make the bet appear safe.

## RELIABILITY:

Weak players = 75 %
Average players = 85 %
Strong players = 60%

## VALUE PER HOUR:

$1 limit = $0.18
$10 limit = $0.83
$100 limit = $1.05

## DISCUSSION:

Suppose you were in a seven-stud game with a king up. There are two other players still to act behind you. You have a king and a queen in the hole, giving you a pair of kings. When the guy with the ten showing starts to bet, does that make you happy or sad? It makes you happy.

But, with poker players being poker players, you can't be 100% sure that the guy will complete this bet. He probably has a pair of tens at best, so you certainly hope he does complete the bet.

What occurs to you, and what occurs to most players, is that it's beneficial to make certain he goes through with the bet. One obvious way of doing this is to start to fold somewhat out of turn. When the bet is made, the player at right will probably act as if he had only been readjusting his card. He'll re-position it and then there's a good chance he'll raise. Except for novices and discourteous opponents, few players pass out of turn when they're weak. That's why if an opponent acts like he's going to pass, you'd better beware.

## BEST STRATEGY:
If you're the man at left, pass.

***Photo 48:***
*While the seven stud player bets (left), his opponent begins to turn his upcard over.*

# TELL #25

**TITLE:**

Maybe I should stand pat on this full house after all.

**CATEGORY:**

Weak Means Strong.

**DESCRIPTION:**

You'll often see inexperienced poker players pretend to draw just before rapping pat. That's exactly what happens in these two photos.

**MOTIVATION:**

An almost instinctive act to confuse the opener.

**RELIABILITY:**

Weak players = 77%
Average players = 59%
Strong players = 54%

**VALUE PER HOUR:**

$1 limit = $0.17
$10 limit = $0.85
$100 limit = $0.90

**DISCUSSION:**

Some players are almost compulsive about disguising their hands. Even if there is little logical benefit in fooling you at the moment, they may still give it a try. When a player who normally doesn't indicate how many he'll draw until it's his turn suddenly decides to let you "know" he needs cards, there's a good chance he'll end up rapping pat. The reason this tell has a fairly low dollar value is because there's very little you can do to capitalize. If you're the opener with a pair of queens, you're going to have to draw three anyway (unless you can split openers and try for a straight or flush). You can gain some ground by knowing that your opponent will probably never rap pat now unless he has a complete hand. He feels that he's made you suspicious and more likely to call by requesting one card out of turn and then changing his mind.

## BEST STRATEGY:

You're playing draw poker with the joker and have asked for one card. You hold.

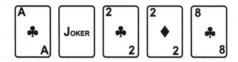

You should consider throwing away the deuce of diamonds and trying for the flush. Even this has disadvantages, because your opponent may have a pat full house and you'll end up drawing dead. If you've asked for three cards to a pair of kings, there's very little you can do at this point; except that if you make three kings and your opponent raps pat, you should not call when he subsequently bets.

***Photo 49:***
*We're playing draw poker. The opener (left) is throwing
away three cards, while an opponent (second from left)
acts as if he's going to discard one.*

***Photo 50:***
*But now that the opener has already received his
three-card draw, his opponent "changes his mind"
and raps pat.*

# TELL #26

## TITLE:
Don't worry about me... yet!

## CATEGORY:
Weak Means Strong.

## DESCRIPTION:
The player (second from left) is betting. What's interesting is that his opponent (center) is looking away from the bet.

## MOTIVATION:
The opponent does not want to discourage or challenge the bettor.

## RELIABILITY:
Weak players = 98%
Average players = 92 %
Strong players = 80%

## VALUE PER HOUR:
$1 limit = $1.85
$10 limit = $10.30
$100 limit = $62.00

## DISCUSSION:
Review this photo carefully. Always keep in mind that players who look away from the action are more dangerous than those who watch or look at the bettor. The man at center does not want to do anything to discourage the bet. Expect him to raise. This is a very important tell.

## BEST STRATEGY:

Don't put any more money into this pot unless you have a very strong hand. If you're the bettor, you should probably abandon your wager now!

***Photo 51:***
*The man in the middle is the one to watch.*

# TELL #27

## TITLE:

I try to look bored before I pounce!

## CATEGORY:

Weak Means Strong.

## DESCRIPTION:

In this sequence, you see that the player in the foreground has picked up a full house, first ace-ace-seven and then ace-seven. That's a terrific hand and, as you'd expect after reading *Chapter 5—Tells From Those Who Are Unaware,* he guards this hand securely. But that's not what we're focusing on here. There's something even more overwhelming happening here. Having secured his aces-full, the player now looks to the left, away from the approaching action.

## MOTIVATION:

He doesn't want to look like a threat.

## RELIABILITY:

Weak players = 92%
Average players = 90%
Strong players = 78%

## VALUE PER HOUR:

$1 limit = $1.00
$10 limit = $5.50
$100 limit = $43.00

## DISCUSSION:

This is similar to the previous tell, except here it's draw poker and the player looks away before the pot is even opened. Coupled with the fact that he guards his hand securely (an *unaware* tell), this is a very predictable situation. The man is acting as if he is uninterested, therefore he's interested. It's that simple.

## BEST STRATEGY:

If you have an opening hand and must act before this player, you should usually check and let him open. If you have only a medium-strength hand, don't play.

***Photo 52:***
*This sequence begins with the draw poker player in the foreground (part of his face at right) picking up.*

***Photo 53:***
*The man in the middle is the one to watch.*

***Photo 54:***
*His whole hand is guarded and he looks away as the action approaches clockwise.*

## PLAY BY PLAY:

Here's a situation similar to the one in the photographs. You're in seat #7.

| MCU Poker Chart | | | | | | | | |
|---|---|---|---|---|---|---|---|---|
| **Game:** Jacks-or-better draw, joker added  **Structure:** $5 ante, $25 bets before draw, $50 after. | | | | | | | | |
| 1 | 2 | 3 | 4 | 5 | 6 | *7* | 8 | Pot |
| a5 | a5 | a5 | a5 | a5 | a5 | a5 | a5 | $40 |
| | | | | | | K♥K K♣K A♠A 2♦2 4♦4 | | Hands before the draw <<< |
| ▲50 | ● — | ▶✔ — | ✔ — | ✔ — | ✔ — | ✔¹ — | 25 =50◀ | $140 |
| 1◀ card | | | | | | | ▶3 cards | |
| + | | | | | | | + | The draw <<< |

| | | | | | | ▶✓ | After the draw <<< |
|---|---|---|---|---|---|---|---|
| 50 | | | | | | =50 ◀ | $240 |
| A♥ A | | | | | | Q♦ Q | |
| 10♣ 10 | | | | | | Q♣ Q | |
| 10♦ 10 | | | | | | 7♠ 7 | |
| 10♥ 10 | | | | | | 4♣ 4 | Hands revealed <<< |
| 4♥ 4 | | | | | | A♣ A | |
| WIN[2] | | | | | | | |

**Chart key:** Action reads left to right, top to bottom. Each betting round begins ▶ with and ends with ◀. Other markings and symbols: a (ante); b (blind bet); ✓ (check); = (call); ▲ (raise); – (fold); ● (dealer position, a.k.a. "the button"). A seat number surrounded by asterisks (for example, *1*) is your seat. Any wager not preceded by a symbol is a voluntary first bet. Wagers indicate the total invested on a betting round. The money in the rightmost column indicates total pot size after the betting.

## MCU POKER CHART NOTES
*(See corresponding numbers within chart.)*

**1)** You're in fifth position. Nobody else has opened. You have a pair of kings and an ace kicker. That ace kicker is important, but not because you have the option of keeping it for deception or to improve your chances of making aces up. Trying for aces-up isn't usually a good idea, because you lessen your chances of making three-of-a kind. The ace is important because it makes it less likely that anyone else holds a pair of aces to beat you.

There are only three players left to act. Kings with an ace (or even without) is usually enough to open with in a jacks-or-better-required-to-open draw poker game, whether or not a joker is added to the deck (as it is in many casinos).

THE TELL. But in this case you've noticed something important about Player #1, who must still act after you. He usually continues to stare at his cards, pretending to be interested, when he's weak. This time he has looked at his cards, closed them quickly and guarded them with his hand. He is now looking *away* from the action as it approaches. This is a powerful signal that Player #1 likes his hand and is pretending to be uninterested. So, instead of opening, you check.

Now, the lady to your left opens. Of course, she gets raised by Player #1, just as you expected. You fold.

**2)** It turns out that Player #1 had three tens. He drew one, keeping an ace kicker to make it look as if he might be trying for a straight or flush. The lady drew three and checked. Player #1 then bet and got called by a pair of queens. You could beat those queens, but you would have lost the pot.

Bottom line: If Player #1 had been as observant as you, she could have folded and saved $100, too.

# TELL #28

**TITLE:**

Don't worry about me... I'm only going to raise!

**CATEGORY:**

Weak Means Strong.

**DESCRIPTION:**

In Photo 55 the woman is studying the flop. Few hold 'em players will watch anything but the board when the dealer spreads the flop. It is a key moment of suspense and it's only human that poker players want to see what comes off the deck. Almost immediately she looks away from the flop, the pot and the action (Photo 56).

**MOTIVATION:**

She likes the flop, but doesn't want to appear threatening.

**RELIABILITY:**

Weak players = 96%
Average players = 94%
Strong players = 77%

**VALUE PER HOUR:**

$1 limit = $1.45
$10 limit = $7.25
$100 limit = $38.00

**DISCUSSION:**

This is a tremendous hold 'em tell. As you've learned, players who look away from the action are giving you profitable information in all forms of poker. But when the flop comes in hold 'em, this tell is especially easy to detect.

## BEST STRATEGY:

Play only very strong hands. If there's a subsequent bet, abandon any hand that you feel would normally be marginal or even slightly profitable. If you have a strong hand, try to let this woman do your betting for you. You dare not bluff.

***Photo 55:***
*It's hold'em and the woman likes the flop.*

***Photo 56:***
*Now she quickly looks away.*

# TELL #29

**TITLE:**

Go ahead and bet your two pair, sucker!

**CATEGORY:**

Weak Means Strong.

**DESCRIPTION:**

Focusing on the player in the foreground (not fully shown), we see that he is hoping for a straight in Photo 57. He makes it in Photo 58, protects his hand in Photo 59 and, finally, acts like he's going to throw his three hole cards away in Photo 60.

**MOTIVATION:**

He feels he has the winning hand and wants to make his opponent's bet seem safe.

**RELIABILITY:**

Weak players = 73 %
Average players = 65%
Strong players = 55%

**VALUE PER HOUR:**

$1 limit = $0.35
$10 limit = $2.10
$100 limit = $8.50

**DISCUSSION:**

It's the last photo that you should concentrate on now. In any type of poker, players who act like they're going to discard their hands before the action reaches them should be considered a threat. There's no reason for them to use this maneuver unless they're trying to fool you. This is definitely a tell where the player is trying to act weak because he is strong. Here, he has a double motive. Not only is he telling his opponent at left that the bet is safe, he's encouraging the other opponent (who must act next) to call.

## BEST STRATEGY:

Abandon all bets! Even if you have a very strong hand, it's usually better to let the man with the straight bet for you. You can later raise with your full house. Don't bluff and don't expect to catch the player in the foreground bluffing. Not this time.

*Photo 57:*
*In the foreground, someone is picking up his final card in seven stud. A five or ten would complete a straight.*

***Photo 58:***
*It's a five.*

***Photo 59:***
*The player carefully places the five with his other two hole cards.*

***Photo 60:***
*While the opponent to his left bets, he acts as if he's going to throw his hand away.*

# TELL #30

## TITLE:
Don't worry about me, I'm not even watching!

## CATEGORY:
Weak Means Strong.

## DESCRIPTION:
Look at the man across the table. This is a very common mannerism. While it's true that most beginners and even some medium level players holding big hands will exaggerate their actions to appear weak, most sophisticated players won't. What you see here is a man acting a little bit weak because he has a strong hand. He's looking away, but only slightly. His mannerism is subtler than the ones we've been studying.

## MOTIVATION:
He doesn't want to discourage your bet.

## RELIABILITY:
Weak players = 80%
Average players = 74%
Strong players = 78%

## VALUE PER HOUR:
$1 limit = $0.15
$10 limit = $7.25
$100 limit = $80.00

## DISCUSSION:
This tell is not much different than a player holding a full house and staring blatantly away from the table. Look

closely and you'll see that the man across the table is looking slightly away as the bet enters the pot. Since he's a sophisticated player, he won't exaggerate this act, but he still applies this universal *Weak Means Strong* trick on a more refined level. He's trying to fool you and he looks ready to pounce... because he *is* ready to pounce.

## BEST STRATEGY:

Don't bet moderately strong hands in the hope of getting a weak call. He doesn't have a weak hand, so a weak call is impossible! You need a big hand to call if he bets. This is not a good opportunity to bluff and you won't *be* bluffed.

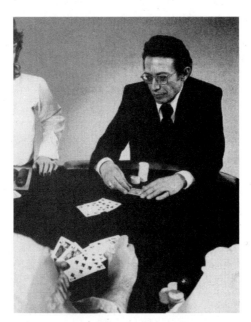

*Photo 61:*
*At bottom left, a man is betting. Across the table, the opponent waits without watching.*

# TELL #31

## TITLE:
How long should I wait before I raise?

## CATEGORY:
Weak Means Strong.

## DESCRIPTION:
In limit poker games, players make their choices promptly. In no-limit games, it's customary to take more time. This is a very important sequence. In Photo 62 the player in the foreground bets, but that's not all! Across the table the opponent makes no movement to prevent the bet. In order to correctly interpret the final strength of the opponent's hand, we must keep this in mind. Even skilled no-limit players will often make some minor gestures to prevent a bet they don't want. They may do this by staring at you, reaching toward their chips or any number of mannerisms to be discussed in the next chapter, *Strong Means Weak*. After the initial bet, the player studies and studies until, in Photo 66, he finally "makes up his mind." Then he moves "all-in" with his chips.

## MOTIVATION:
The long hesitation is designed to make the original bettor think that the raise is a tough decision.

## RELIABILITY:
Weak players = 80%
Average players = 75 %
Strong players = 65%

## VALUE PER HOUR:
small no-limit = $ 1.85
medium no-limit = $12.00
large no-limit = $90.00

## DISCUSSION:
When a no-limit player does nothing to discourage a sizable bet, then hesitates for a long time and chooses to make a large raise, there's little chance that he's bluffing. His long delay is an effort to make you think his raise is marginal and therefore weak. Some professionals may argue that *any* player who makes a large raise is likely to have a very strong hand whether he hesitates long or not. While this may be true, it's also a fact that a player is *even more* likely to have a winning hand if he takes longer than an average amount of time to act. Remember, though, in no-limit poker an *average amount of time* can be half a minute or more, whereas in limit games most decisions require only a few seconds.

## BEST STRATEGY:
The flop is four of diamonds, eight of spades, jack of diamonds. If you were the bettor in the left foreground, you would need a very strong hand to call the raise. As an example, you might need two eights (giving you three eights) to consider calling. That's because the best hand you could beat would be two fours (giving your opponent three fours). And two fours might be the minimum raising hand of some conservative opponents. You must ask yourself whether this opponent would have risked moving all-in with a jack and an eight (making two big pair) or a jack and a four. Liberal players might even raise all-in with a pair of aces or an ace of diamonds with an eight of diamonds. But, in that case, it's unlikely they'd perform

the long *act* of deciding. If a raise truly is marginal, players are generally hesitant to let you know it. Here's an opportunity to earn a profit by throwing away some pretty good hands. Remember, what you save by not calling this raise is real money and it can buy real things.

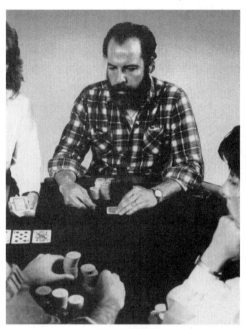

***Photo 62:***
*It's no limit hold 'em and the man in the foreground is betting.*

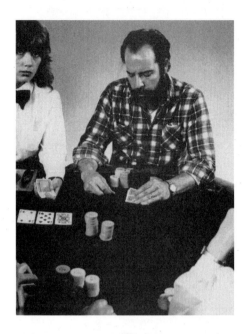

***Photo 63:***
*The player across
the table begins to
consider.*

***Photo 64:***
*Ten seconds pass
and he's still
considering.*

***Photo 65:***
*Now he puts a finger*
*to his head to help*
*his concentration.*

***Photo 66:***
*Decision finally*
*made, he gestures,*
*"I've got it!"*

***Photo 67:***
*He reaches for his stacks...*

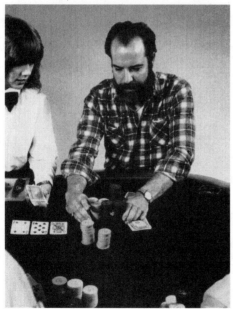

***Photo 68:***
*...and bets everything!*

# Strong Means Weak

I often teach my students to concentrate on this aspect of tells first. In a poker game, the urge to act strong when weak can be overpowering for most players. It's reverse—weak when strong, which we've just studied—is also widespread.

You've seen, in terms of dollars, how much you can earn every hour by catching strong players in their tireless act of pretending to be weak.

But catching players who are pretending to be strong is even more valuable. The reason is simple. If you use the science of tells to determine that a player is strong, you'll often end up passing when you otherwise might have called. In a typical limit game, a pot may be $100 large and it would cost you $20 to call. If you discover that your opponent has a strong hand, you'll be able to fold with confidence. The most you will earn on a single tell is probably $20, the size of the saved bet. Of course, you can occasionally save two or more bets by folding even earlier in the hand. But, in an example where you're focusing on one late bet and deciding whether or not to call, $20 is usually the most you can save by correctly throwing your hand away.

It turns out that your *actual* savings is *less* than $20. That's because you might have decided to pass without even observing the tell. The tell is not apt to be 100%

accurate, so it might sometimes cause you to throw away a *winning* hand when you might otherwise have called. All in all, the information you gain by observing tells is healthy for your bankroll, but you must be aware that the theoretical value of each tell-related decision is apt to be only a percentage of what you think it is.

When you determine that a player is acting weak when strong, you'll often save a call, but the value is usually only a theoretical portion of the bet. It's a different story if you catch a player acting strong when weak. You will often use that information to make a courageous call you would not otherwise have considered. In such a case, you will frequently win an *entire pot* you would have lost!

Before going forward, it's a good time to remind you that the dollar values given for each tell should be carefully interpreted. First, remember that the value is only an approximation and may vary from game to game. Second, it represents the *maximum you* could earn on that specific tell if you spotted it every time it occurred. In practice, nobody can be aware of everything that goes on at a poker table. Third, in some respects the dollar value is *greater* than you'd think, because the value provided applies to the specific tell under scrutiny and does not include related tells suggested by the same mannerism.

Now let's discover a vastly important category of tells. Never forget that players will not waste energy making you think they're strong when they really are. Why should they?

---

*Caro's Law of Tells #12*
*Disappoint any player who, by acting strong,*
*is hoping you'll pass.*

---

# TELL #32

## TITLE:
If these cards change, I'll be a witness.

## CATEGORY:
Strong Means Weak.

## DESCRIPTION:
The player's eyes fix on the flop in Photo 69. That doesn't tell us much, because almost all hold 'em players watch the flop. But in Photo 70 the player's eyes remain on the flop, and that fact could be important.

## MOTIVATION:
He's trying to appear dangerous by showing interest in the flop.

## RELIABILITY:
Weak players = 72 %
Average players = 65 %
Strong players = 55%

## VALUE PER HOUR:
$1 limit = $1.40
$10 limit = $2.90
$100 limit = $14.00

## DISCUSSION:
Players have a habit of continuing to stare at a flop they don't like. In their mind, by pretending to be interested, they're discouraging opponents from betting. It may even work—except against you. Being educated in the science

of tells, you realize that players who like flops are likely to look away. If you notice that sometimes a player turns his head quickly away from the flop and sometimes he doesn't, you can figure he's weak whenever he continues to stare.

## BEST STRATEGY:

Here's a good bluffing opportunity for you. Also, if this guy bets, you should call more liberally than usual, because there's a large chance that he's weak or bluffing.

*Photo 69:*
*The hold 'em player at left watches as the flop is spread.*

*Photo 70:*
*His eyes remain on the flop.*

# TELL #33

## TITLE:
Watch me make a fist.

## CATEGORY:
Strong Means Weak.

## DESCRIPTION:
Many novice players, and some intermediate players, try to fool the opposition by gesturing to rap pat before it's their turn. You can see the player second from right performing this act. There is no penalty for changing his mind, because general poker rules dictate that "acting out of turn is not binding."

## MOTIVATION:
He hopes the opener will be mislead.

## RELIABILITY:
Weak players = 88%
Average players = 68%
Strong players = 56%

## VALUE PER HOUR:
$1 limit = $0.18
$10 limit = $1.10
$100 limit = $9.50

## DISCUSSION:
Even if you can interpret this tell correctly, it seldom does you much good in high-hand-wins draw poker. True, the opponent is trying to mislead you by pretending to rap pat, but his motive is fairly hazy. He wants to fool you, but

in his heart he doesn't quite know why. You can be fairly certain that he'll draw cards, but what can you do about it? In lowball, the tell is more beneficial.

## BEST STRATEGY:

If an opponent is pretending to rap pat behind you and your jacks-or-better-to-open hand is...

...you should definitely draw three to the aces and not be tricked into splitting openers and trying for the flush. If the game is lowball, there's a much greater chance that you can earn a profit here. If you have a hand such as 9-7-6-4-2 and were tempted to draw one, you should now rap pat, knowing that your lowball opponent will be drawing cards.

*Photo 71:*
*It's draw poker. The opener (second from left) is drawing a card, while an opponent seems to be rapping pat.*

# TELL #34

## TITLE:

I'm watching, so you better know what you're doing.

## CATEGORY:

Strong Means Weak.

## DESCRIPTION:

Keep in mind that players looking *at* the bettor are typically less of a threat than players looking *away.* Here, the player at center is watching the bet.

## MOTIVATION:

By appearing interested, he's trying to tell his opponent that a bet is not safe.

## RELIABILITY:

Weak players = 70%
Average players = 65 %
Strong players = 58%

## VALUE PER HOUR:

$1 limit = $1.30
$10 limit = $9.85
$100 limit = $58.50

## DISCUSSION:

While this is a fairly powerful tell, it has its problems. It's clear that players who stare at you are generally weaker than those who stare away. But it so happens that, especially in limit games, there's a secondary reason why opponents watch your bet: They want to make sure you wager the right amount, so they won't get short-changed. You can sometimes be fooled into thinking an opponent is trying to act strong when, in fact, he's only monitoring the size of your bet. This tell poses that dilemma. If the player (center) was looking directly at the bettor's face, we'd have no problem. In such a case, it would be fairly clear that the bet was unwelcome. Even in this photo, however, you can assume that the opponent watching the bet is not *usually* strong. Just for contrast, look at Photo 51 in Section XII, *Weak Means Strong*.

## BEST STRATEGY:

You can bet medium-strength hands into the player at center with the hope of getting a call from a weaker hand. Also, if you hold a hopeless hand, you might try bluffing.

*Caro's Law of Tells #13*
*Players staring at you are usually less*
*of a threat than players staring away.*

*Photo 72:*
*Watch the man at center as his opponent*
*(second from left) wagers.*

# TELL #35

## TITLE:

I'll just keep staring until they get better.

## CATEGORY:

Strong Means Weak.

## DESCRIPTION:

If you've been in draw poker games against weak players, you've probably observed this. The player would normally guard his hand if he liked its looks. Now, however, he just stares at the cards as they arrive and, finally, in Photo 75 he reaches for his chips as if to bet.

## MOTIVATION:

He's hoping players with medium hands will decide not to open. (If no one opens in jacks-or-better draw, there's traditionally a second ante and all players get a new chance at the pot.)

## RELIABILITY:

Weak players = 88%
Average players = 73%
Strong players = 62%

## VALUE PER HOUR:

$1 limit = $2.74
$10 limit = $18.50
$100 limit = $128.00

## DISCUSSION:

In jacks-or-better-to-open draw poker, each player gets

a chance to open the pot. If nobody opens, the antes remain in the pot and new antes are usually added. Then there's a brand new deal and everyone gets a second opportunity to win. If you held a garbage hand, obviously it would be to your advantage if no one opened. And that's exactly how the guy (right foreground) has it figured. By reaching for his chips out of turn and staring at his cards, he's hoping to convince his opponents that he's a threat. Maybe that will prevent them from opening with marginal hands. This seldom works, but players try it anyway. The information you gain by observing their futile attempts can be very valuable. For comparison, see Photos 52, 53 and 54 in Section XII, *Weak Means Strong.*

## BEST STRATEGY:

Not only should you go right ahead and open with any hand that seems marginal, you should open with some hands you might otherwise not have considered. The reason is that, in all forms of poker, the more players remaining to act behind you, the more jeopardy you're in. The fewer players remaining, the more liberally you can open. When you see a player behind you stare at his cards and reach for his chips, you should act as if he isn't there! You have fewer players to contend with and you can profit with hands you would not have played.

---

### Caro's Law of Tells #14
*Players staring at their cards are usually weak.*

---

### Caro's Law of Tells #15
*Players reaching for their chips out of turn are usually weak.*

---

***Photo 73:***
*It's draw poker, high hand wins, and the player at right foreground picks up three awful-looking cards.*

***Photo 74:***
*Continuing to gaze at the first three cards held in his left hand, he picks up two more terrible cards.*

***Photo 75:***
*He now stares at all five cards and reaches for his chips.*

# TELL #36

## TITLE:
I thought you already passed.

## CATEGORY:
Strong Means Weak.

## DESCRIPTION:
Here the bettor is reaching for the chips before her opponent has surrendered.

## MOTIVATION:
She wants to show strength by indicating that the outcome is a sure thing.

## RELIABILITY:
Weak players = 85 %
Average players = 81%
Strong players = 54%

## VALUE PER HOUR:
$1 limit = $0.90
$10 limit = $8.10
$100 limit = $7.50

## DISCUSSION:
Strong players sometimes reach for the pot prematurely as a ploy to induce a call. (That's why this tell has a small proportional value in big-limit games.) Often, this is done ostentatiously while an opponent is just beginning to consider. However, when a player reaches for the pot while the opponent is *in the act of passing,* the interpretation is

different. Usually, the bettor wants to ensure that the pot is won by driving the last tiny doubts from the mind of an already-passing opponent. While this may be difficult to conceptualize at first, consider that any player who truly holds a winning hand would give you every opportunity to call. If this woman wanted a call, she wouldn't reach for the pot until there was no chance whatsoever that you might change your mind.

## BEST STRATEGY:

If you were about to throw your hand away, consider calling—even with a fairly weak hand. And if you have a hand so horrible that you can't beat anything, try raising as a bluff. Here's a chance to snare a whole pot that would have got away.

---

*Carols Law of Tells #16*
*A weak player who gathers a pot prematurely*
*is usually bluffing.*

---

*Photo 76:*
*The woman has bet and now, while the opponent at left is still in the act of passing, she begins to gather the pot.*

# TELL #37

**TITLE:**
Are you sure you want to call these?

**CATEGORY:**
Strong Means Weak.

**DESCRIPTION:**
Here we see a bet made in Photo 77. In Photo 78, the bettor stares at his cards. When his opponent begins to call, in Photo 79, the bettor quickly acts as if to spread a winning hand.

**MOTIVATION:**
He's desperately hoping to prevent the call.

**RELIABILITY:**
Weak players = 99%
Average players = 89 %
Strong players = 78%

**VALUE PER HOUR:**
$1 limit = $1.32
$10 limit = $9.04
$100 limit = $52.00

**DISCUSSION:**
As a last futile, desperate effort to prevent a call, many players will start to spread a bluff (or a weak hand) on the table. You can actually elicit this tell by reaching for your chips and then gauging the reaction of a player who has bet into you. If he starts to spread his hand prematurely,

you can be pretty certain that you can profitably make the call. I like to apply this tactic when I'm leaning toward passing. If I reach for my chips and the bettor starts to spread his hand, I'll just continue to make the call smoothly. Otherwise, I'll pass. Often you can salvage an entire pot because a player will apply this fairly common mannerism in an attempt to prevent you from betting.

## BEST STRATEGY:
Call. And if you can't win calling, raise.

---

### *Caro's Law of Tells #17*
*When a player acts to spread his hand prematurely,*
*it's usually because he's bluffing.*

---

***Photo 77:***
*The player in the hat wagers, while his*
*opponent (left) waits.*

***Photo 78:***
*The bettor now stares at his hand.*

***Photo 79:***
*As the opponent begins to call, the bettor starts to
spread his hand on the table.*

# TELL #38

## TITLE:
Drawing for a straight! How can you bet?

## CATEGORY:
Strong Means Weak.

## DESCRIPTION:
I bet you've seen this before. The seven-stud player in the foreground tries for a straight in Photo 80, misses in Photo 81 and reaches for his chips while staring at his hole cards in Photo 82.

## MOTIVATION:
He's hoping to prevent the bet in progress.

## RELIABILITY:
Weak players = 93%
Average players = 84 %
Strong players = 72%

## VALUE PER HOUR:
$1 limit = $1.55
$10 limit = $9.00
$100 limit = $96.00

## DISCUSSION:
Staring at seven-stud hole cards is somewhat rare in public casinos, but it happens a lot in home games. The more important thing to focus on is that the player in the foreground is reaching for his chips. You should already understand that the gesture is purely an effort to prevent a bet. There are all sorts of applications of the tell pictured,

depending on whether you're the bettor or the man to the dealer's right. But wait! There's another terrific tell that you might have missed. The player to the dealer's right is looking back at his cards while the bet is in progress. This almost always means weakness!

Players with strong hands may occasionally double-check, but only briefly. If a player who was *not already* staring at his cards begins to do so in the middle of an opponent's bet, he's doing it because he wants to be seen. Specifically, he's hoping to appear threatening. We can carry this concept further. If someone has bet and then looks back at his cards as you reach toward your chips to call, there's an overwhelming chance that he's bluffing.

## BEST STRATEGY:

If you're the bettor, continue with the wager. You might get called by the player in the foreground who missed the straight (he also has a pair of nines). Alternately, you might choose to check if you think that the chances of gaining a call are slim but that one of your opponents might try to bluff. You could then call and win an extra bet.

---

### Caro's Law of Tells #18
*If a player bets and then looks back at his hand as you reach for your chips, he's probably bluffing.*

---

***Photo 80:***
*The seven stud player in the foreground requires a 10 or a 5 to complete a straight.*

***Photo 81:***
*No help.*

***Photo 82:***
*As an opponent bets, the player stares at his hole cards and reaches for his chips.*

# Exposing Cards

Careless players sometimes expose cards by accident. This usually happens when they aren't interested in the pot. A player who's involved in a betting war or is otherwise competing for a pot will usually guard a hand carefully. When you see a player expose one or more strong cards, beware! Also, though this is rare, a player may expose a weak card when he holds a powerful hand. In either case, the exposure is seldom accidental.

You can correctly suppose that a player who deliberately exposes a strong card or several strong cards is actually weak. Let's take a look...

# TELL #39

## TITLE:
Try figuring out what three cards I'm keeping.

## CATEGORY:
Exposing Cards.

## DESCRIPTION:
This is draw poker with a pair of jacks minimum required to open. The player in the center is the opener. His opponent, who first passed and later called the opening bet, is at left. When this photo was taken, the caller had already drawn three cards, probably to a pair smaller than jacks. The opener is now drawing two cards while "accidentally" exposing a ten.

## MOTIVATION:
He wants to make his opponent think he has three tens.

## RELIABILITY:
Weak players = 92%
Average players = 83%
Strong players = 71%

## VALUE PER HOUR:
$1 limit = $0.30
$10 limit = $1.50
$100 limit = $~.80

## DISCUSSION:
The opener is hoping that the caller will use some simple logic. Since at least a pair of jacks is required to open, it

seems more likely that the exposed ten indicates three tens than a higher pair with a ten kicker. But if this guy really had three tens, he wouldn't want to let anyone know—especially his opponent. Rather, he'd hope the opponent would help his small pair (making three eights, for instance) and then call. It's important to understand what the opener seeks to accomplish. He probably holds a pair of jacks, queens or kings and doesn't want the opponent to bet two pair or even three of a kind.

If the opponent improves and doesn't bet, the opener may still lose the pot, but it won't cost him any more money. This whole act of exposing a ten is designed to stop the opponent from betting. Therefore, the exposed ten is intended as a *strong* card, which you know means the opposite.

Under other circumstances, if the opponent hadn't first passed and then "backed in" to call, the opener might suspect the caller has a better hand than his weak openers. In such a case, he might expose the ten and then *bet,* hoping the opponent would throw away the better hand. In this photo, he will no doubt check unless he improves. Remember, the opener figures to have the best hand so far, but it's a vulnerable hand and he doesn't want to have to consider calling a bet.

## BEST STRATEGY:

What can I tell you? If you're the player at left and called with a pair of eights, you probably made a mistake! Calling with a small pair is simply not profitable in most situations. Still, here you are contending for the pot, so what can you do now? Well, if the opener checks and you make *any* two pair, you should bet. A bet is what the opener is trying to prevent, so why make him happy? Also, this is a very good bluffing opportunity if you *don't* help your hand.

***Photo 83:***
*The player at center is asking for two cards and exposing
a ten among the three cards he's keeping.*

# TELL #40

## TITLE:
It's too much trouble betting with my left hand.

## CATEGORY:
Exposing Cards.

## DESCRIPTION:
The player in the foreground is holding his cards in the same hand he's using to make his bet. This causes the "accidental" exposure of the joker.

## MOTIVATION:
He wants to convey strength.

## RELIABILITY:
Weak players = 84%
Average players = 75%
Strong players = 61%

## VALUE PER HOUR:
$1 limit = $0.90
$10 limit = $3.00
$100 limit = $14.00

## DISCUSSION:
The inclusion of the joker, making the deck 53 cards deep, is common in draw poker. Sometimes the joker is considered a wild card which can represent anything the holder desires; sometimes (as with legal games in California) it's limited to use as an ace or to complete a straight or a flush. In any case, it's a powerful card. Ask

yourself why an opponent would want to expose a joker while betting. There's something wrong, isn't there? He must be attempting to trick you into thinking he's strong when he's weak. This is probably a bluff.

## BEST STRATEGY:
Call.

***Photo 84:***
*The player in the foreground bets and simultaneously exposes the joker.*

# Opening Tells

Determining who's going to open a pot and who isn't is one of the most profitable applications of tells. In games where you can check and later call or raise, there's seldom a reason for you to make the first bet if someone else will do it for you.

The advantages in knowing whether someone intends to open are many. If you were considering playing a weak hand, you can bow out gracefully by simply checking and later passing. If you have a strong hand, it's usually better to check, let the opponent open and see how many callers there are by the time the action returns to your position. At that point you can either call or raise. In fact, there may be several raises by the time the action returns, and this may indicate your hand is not worth playing. In such a case, you can pass without losing even an opening bet.

Opening tells are extremely powerful in many forms of poker. They are most common in draw poker games. That's because in high-hand wins draw poker, there's an incentive for players to disguise their hands even if they have no chance of winning. If nobody opens, the original ante is not lost—there is a double ante and a new deal. That's motive enough for players who are holding weak hands to pretend to be strong, thereby keeping you from opening.

Here are seven players.

# TELL #41

**TITLE:**
To open or not to open...

**CATEGORY:**
Opening Tells.

**DESCRIPTION:**
It's draw poker, jacks-or-better to open. The player in the foreground (left) holds three aces, but he'd just as soon let someone else open. Someone will. Which player is it?

**MOTIVATION:**
The player who will open is trying to appear as if he isn't a threat.

**RELIABILITY:**
Weak players = 98%
Average players = 91%
Strong players = 80%

**VALUE PER HOUR:**
$1 limit = $2.18
$10 limit = $11.20
$100 limit = $85.00

**DISCUSSION:**
It's up to the player holding three aces to either check or open. He wants to know if anyone else will bet for him, so let's go clockwise around the table and find out. First, there's a man who's reaching for his chips out of turn. He's trying to suggest he has a hand strong enough to open; therefore he probably doesn't. Then there's a woman staring

at her cards, trying to make us think they're powerful. Since strong means weak, she must have less than the minimum pair of jacks required to open. Next, a man is gazing away from the action and even pretending to throw his hand away. There's an overwhelming chance that he'll open. Weak means strong, remember. If you hold the three aces, you'd know not to open because this man will do it for you. The last three players are all staring at their cards and probably have weak hands.

## BEST STRATEGY:

If you have the three aces in the foreground, check and let the man in the leather jacket open. By the way, his mannerisms suggest that he has a pretty powerful hand, so deciding whether you should raise or just call will be difficult.

*Photo 85:*
*The cards have just been dealt and these seven players are competing for the jacks-or-better pot.*

# Encouraging Your Bet

When players encourage your bet, it's because they think they have a winning hand. Some of the usual ways of luring bets are not visual, but audible. They're related to the act of conveying weakness through tone of voice, sighs and other sounds. We'll deal with that in *Chapter 8—The Sounds of Tells*.

The most common visual methods opponents use to make your bet appear safe are: (1) Looking away as if uninterested; (2) Pretending to pass; and (3) Keeping their hands off their chips.

# TELL #42

**TITLE:**

I wonder if it's raining in Cincinnati.

**CATEGORY:**

Encouraging Your Bet.

**DESCRIPTION:**

At left, a man is considering his bet. At center, an opponent studies seriously. Focus on the man at right. He's acting as if he isn't even involved. Maybe you don't consider him a threat, but you should.

**MOTIVATION:**

The man at right wants to do nothing to interfere with a possible bet.

**RELIABILITY:**

Weak players = 96%
Average players = 91%
Strong players = 69%

**VALUE PER HOUR:**

$1 limit = $2.04
$10 limit = $14.60
$100 limit = $95.00

**DISCUSSION:**

Since the man at center looks so studious, you should figure that he doesn't have a powerhouse. If he did, he'd be apt to encourage your bet by appearing uninterested. Here he either has a genuine tough decision or he's trying to intimidate his opponent into passing. Yes, close scrutiny can be intimidating. The man at right is strong. Whenever you see an active player looking as if the pot is far from his mind. . . well, that's a dangerous opponent. In all probability, he's hoping for a bet and, in response, he'll raise.

## BEST STRATEGY:

Pass, unless you have a powerful hand. Even then, you should probably check and let him do the betting. Don't bluff.

***Photo 86:***
*The player at left is considering a bet, while one man studies and another looks bored.*

## PLAY BY PLAY:

Although the photo uses seven-card stud as an example game, this tell is very common in all forms of poker. Lets look at a hold 'em example of taking advantage of an opponent *acting* distracted. You're in seat #5.

## MCU Poker Chart

*Game:* Hold 'em  *Structure:* $25 and $50 blinds, $50 bets on starting hand and flop, $100 thereafter.

| 1 | 2 | 3 | 4 | *5* | 6 | 7 | 8 | 9 | 10 | Pot |
|---|---|---|---|---|---|---|---|---|---|---|
| | | ● | b25 | b50 | | | | | | $75 |
| | | | | K♥K / K♦K | | | | | | **Starting hands** <<< |
| | | | | | ▶100 | — | — | =100 | — | $925 |
| =100 | — | =100 | — | ▲150[1] | =150 | | | ▲200[2] | | |
| — | | =200 | | =200 | =200◀ | | | | | |
| | | | | | | | | | | **Flop** K♠K / 8♥8 / 10♠10 <<< $1,325 |
| | | =100[3] | ▶50 | =100[4] | =50 =100◀ | | | ▲100 | | |
| | | =100 =200◀ | | ▶♥[5] ▲200 | ♥[6] =200 | | | 100 =200 | | **Turn** 8♠8 <<< $2,125 |
| | | =100 =300 =400◀ | | ▶♥[7] ▲200 ▲400 | 100 ▲300 =400 | | | =100 — | | **River** 9♠9 <<< $3,425 |
| | | Q♣Q / J♦J | | K♥K / K♦K WIN | 9♦9 / 9♣9 | | | | | **Two-card hands revealed** <<< |

> **Chart key:** Action reads left to right, top to bottom. Each betting round begins ▶ with and ends with ◀ . Other markings and symbols: a (ante); b (blind bet); ✔ (check); = (call); ▲ (raise); – (fold); ● (dealer position, a.k.a. "the button"). A seat number surrounded by asterisks (for example, *1*) is your seat. Any wager not preceded by a symbol is a voluntary first bet. Wagers indicate the total invested on a betting round. The money in the rightmost column indicates total pot size after the betting.

## MCU POKER CHART NOTES

*(See corresponding numbers within chart.)*

**1)** Let me look at this chart for a second. OK, you're in Seat #5 and you have the big blind. The guy immediately to your left raises to $100. His name is Sam and you like to play with him because he's extremely easy to read. Some players are much more valuable to you in giving away tells—and Sam is in one of the more profitable categories. Anyway, you think Sam is raising with a reasonable hand. Sure enough, he has a pocket pair of nines, but you don't know this yet. Seat #9 calls, as do seats #1 and #3.

You have a pair of kings. Now you can make an argument for just calling in this situation, but most of the time you should raise and get full value, which is what you decide to do. Calling has the advantage of maintaining deception, because opponents think that a player in the big blind might call with almost anything. But with four other players already committed to $100, this raise is very profitable. You almost certainly have the best hand to this point, and four more $50 calls means $200 out of which you're earning a decent percentage—in the long run. Another powerful reason why you should usually raise in this situation is that if you just call there is no possibility of any extra action. Had Sam in seat #6 and Beatrice in seat #9 just called your big blind and *then* seat #1 had raised, this would be an entirely different scenario. In that case, you could more strongly consider just calling. That decision would tend to keep the $50 callers from being scared away by having to call a double raise. And the possibility of being reraised again, keeping the action going, would exist. In other words, your call wouldn't close the betting.

You can make a strong argument, of course, that you should raise in that situation, because you *want* to chase those players out and leave their surrendered money in the pot to be fought over by you and just two other opponents. That's a good argument, and whether it's true or not is a strategic consideration that is beyond the scope of this book—which is mostly about tells. And, in any case, that's not what happened. Sam raised right away and everyone called his raise. It's back to you in the big blind and I would recommend a $50 raise to $150 total. That's what you did, so we're all satisfied.

**2)** After Sam calls the raise, suddenly Beatrice in seat #9 makes it $200. That's the "cap" in this game, meaning no more raises are allowed (three maximum, which is traditional in many casinos). Although Beatrice won't make it to the showdown, I'll give you a little magic information: She holds ace and king of clubs. Is that worth another reraise here? Or should she have just called. Actually, she should scramble the decision in similar situations. Sometimes raise, sometimes just call the $150. If it were me, I would usually just call and raise only rarely.

Faced with calling a double raise, seat #1 gives up, but everyone else calls, including seat #3 who has a queen-jack. If you believe typical players always surrender this hand, you need to reevaluate how real people actually play. Most are considerably more frivolous with their calls than you might imagine, and this hand isn't anything that would routinely be folded, even against several raises. The call of the first raise was merely worth a yawn. Often this player would fold when faced with two more raises after his first call, but he figures, "What the heck, it's already capped. What's another $100?"

It's time for the flop. Nice flop, huh? You now have three kings and there's no straight or flush possible yet. In other words, we know—since the king is the high communal card on board—that you hold absolutely, positively the best hand right now. You're first to act and you decide to bet. That's OK, although you might argue for a check-raise. After all, sandbagging is always a better idea when you're not the one who bet last on the previous round. It was Beatrice who bet last by capping the raises. Anyway, it's done now, so let's see what happens. Sam calls in seat #6, but he seems genuinely hesitant to do it. Beatrice raises. She's made top pair with an ace kicker.

**3)** Seat #3 calls the raise with queen-jack. This guy came to play and he flopped an open-end straight draw. Why not?

**4)** And you just call. Hmm… Well, OK, I know what you're thinking. Try a little deception here. Why chase Sam out with a double raise? I don't know, I probably would have raised, but your call is a reasonable alternative—as long as you don't "slow play" hands like that too often.

Sam calls, ending the action. The turn card is now dealt. It's an eight of spades, giving you kings full and making a flush possible for your opponents. Now you decide to check. A check here makes sense because you didn't raise on the flop. Had you raised at that point, a check now might have seemed stranger and more suspicious. As it is, your check seems like the most natural thing in the world. A slight problem with it is that the person immediately to your left isn't the likely bettor. In fact, Sam—who is to your left in seat #6—reached toward his chips as you were deciding what to do. As you saw elsewhere in this book, that's almost a sure sign that Sam is *not* going to bet. It's a defensive ploy on his part, designed to keep *you* from betting. And, sure enough, Sam checks right after you do.

Whenever you sandbag (check-raise) from strength, it's better if the player immediately after you bets. That way, you can get a lot of callers and *then* raise. If players immediately after you also check and then someone else raises, you face a dilemma when the action returns to you. Do you raise with your almost-certain winning hand, making the opponents to your left face a double raise, and risk losing them? Or do you seethe silently and just call? Always remember that it's better to sandbag a powerful hand when the player immediately to your left is the likely bettor.

Conversely, if you want to chase players *out* of the pot with a medium-strong hand, then it's better if the player immediately to your right is the bettor—because that player will act last. You check. Everyone else checks to the player on your right. He bets. You raise. Now everyone else is forced either to call a double raise or to fold—and you're likely to reduce the field.

In this case, it wasn't the most-desirable player immediately to your left who was the most likely bettor; it was the *second* player to your left. So, you decided to check, and that was a reasonable decision. Too bad that Sam checked, but that was what you expected from the reach-toward-chips tell.

Now we get to the next action, and Beatrice decides to bet her ace-king (remember, the chart doesn't show you her cards because she doesn't reach the showdown, but I previously told you what she holds). Normally, that bet could be a solid decision, but in this case she has no chance of winning whatsoever. Seat #3 decides to call, hoping for an ace or a nine on the river to make a straight.

**5)** You raise. This is probably your best choice now. It's the reason you checked to begin with. You might lose Sam to your left, because he faces a double raise, but you'll probably get called by Beatrice in seat #9 and by seat #3.

**6)** Ah, but Sam *does* call the double raise. As you can see if you jump ahead to the showdown, he holds a pair of nines. Would *you* call with that hand? Probably not, but if you're surprised that Sam or millions of players like him would call, you haven't yet gained a solid understanding about how many opponents play. Players like Sam will sometimes surrender this hand and sometimes call with it. The decision is mostly by whim.

The other two players call.

**7)** A nine of spades falls on the river.

THE TELL. Glancing out of the corner of your eyes, you see that Sam's demeanor has suddenly changed. He's looking up and away, seeming distracted, as he waits for you to act on your hand. Does this mean he's lost interest in the pot? That nine of spades could have provided him with a flush. But, wait! He's acting *really* uninterested. That's the tell given by someone who is waiting to pounce and doesn't want to do anything to discourage your bet. He's *acting* weak; he's actually strong. Could he have made a full house, you wonder?

Whatever he has, it's that last card that helped him. He could have played a queen-jack and connected for a straight on the river. But then he would have felt vulnerable and afraid of a flush, because there are four spades showing.

Flush? It would have to be a big one. You probably wouldn't see this tell unless Sam had the ace of spades for a nut flush. Full house? The more you think about it, the more you wonder if Sam holds a pair of nines and *that's* how the final nine helped him.

But, in any case, it looks like Sam feels confident about his hand and wants to bet. So, using this powerful tell as your guide, you check. Just like you thought, Sam bets.

Beatrice calls with her ace-king (top pair and an ace kicker). Seat #3 calls, holding queen-jack for a straight. Sure looks like an awfully weak call, doesn't it? Now you raise. If it were possible, you would like to just call and let Sam raise, but that *isn't* possible, because Sam was the first bettor. If you just call now the betting will be over. Now Sam raises again. Beatrice with top pair and an ace kicker finally folds. But, gosh, seat #3 with a seemingly hopeless straight—in the face of easy flush and even full-house possibilities—calls both raises! What is he thinking?

Well, he's not. He's caught up in the moment. Players get this way some times. They make foolish calls in the heat of poker combat that they would not make if they could lean back and think rationally. Seat #3 is better than a lot of players, though, and would probably throw this hand away most of the time. But right now, he's shell-shocked. Too many chips coming from too many places and he's lost his logic. It happens. You now cap it, putting in the final allowable raise. Sam calls. Seat #3 hesitates, realizing he has no rational chance of winning, but calls the final $100, anyway. He can't help himself.

Now the showdown. Your kings full beats Sam's nines full and seat #3's straight. Nice play. Had you not spotted the tell, you might have bet on the river, because you were the last raiser on the previous betting round. (Of course, a check would have looked fairly natural, too, because it looks like you may be suddenly worried about a flush. After all, someone's likely to have spade—which is all it takes to make a flush with four spades on the board.) If you had bet, Sam would have raised, and Beatrice probably would have folded immediately. You made $900 from opponents on the final betting round. But you probably would have made $800 or less (depending on what seat #3 would have done facing a double raise with no river-round chips "invested" yet) if you hadn't spotted the tell.

Let's figure the average profit from spotting the tell in this unusual situation is $120. That illustrates the value of tells. These opportunities surround you in poker.

# TELL #43

**TITLE:**

Can't you see I'm going to pass?

**CATEGORY:**

Encouraging Your Bet.

**DESCRIPTION:**

In the previous tell, you saw a man looking away. This man is also looking away, but, additionally, he's getting ready to throw his cards away. Or so you're supposed to presume.

**MOTIVATION:**

He's hungry for your bet.

**RELIABILITY:**

Weak players = 100%
Average players = 94%
Strong players = 90%

**VALUE PER HOUR:**

$1 limit = $3.50
$10 limit = $20.40
$100 limit = $185.00

**DISCUSSION:**

There's not much to say here. Study that man across the table. He's looking away *and* beginning to pass out of turn. This is an outstanding example of what real-life players do to encourage your bet. Whenever you see this, you're in a lot more trouble than you can itemize.

## BEST STRATEGY:

Don't bet. When he bets, pass. Don't bluff. Don't expect to catch him bluffing. One note about finesse: Since this tell is so valuable, you should not pass instantly. Your decision is obvious, but don't make it *seem* obvious to your opponent. If you do, he might change his behavior and provide fewer tells in the future. If you hesitate before making your decision, he'll figure that his act almost worked— and he may even exaggerate it the next time.

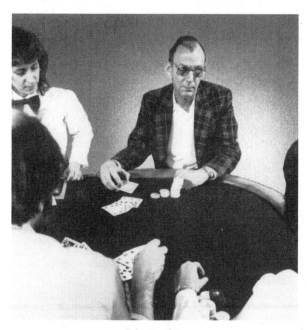

***Photo 87:***
*The player in the right foreground is betting.*
*Is the bet safe?*

# TELL #44

**TITLE:**
Never worry about a girl like me.

**CATEGORY:**
Encouraging Your Bet.

**DESCRIPTION:**
While the man bets, the woman in the black sweater very subtly stares at the table, unwilling to move. Her left hand provides a slight hint that she might be passing. Motivation: She doesn't want to discourage the bet.

**RELIABILITY:**
Weak players = 88%
Average players = 80 %
Strong players = 72%

**VALUE PER HOUR:**
$1 limit = $2.08
$10 limit = $11.00
$100 limit = $50.00

**DISCUSSION:**
It would be nice if all tells were as blatant as those shown in the two previous photos. Many are, but some are much more subtle. Take Photo 88, for instance. This is composed of the same elements that made up the previous tell. But here it's harder to spot. The woman is looking away, but she isn't gazing off the table or into space. She's simply looking down. Don't be fooled into thinking she's staring at her chips. Instinctive glances at chips, which we've already studied, are extremely brief, and they occur when your opponent is not aware that you're looking. In

any case, they lead you to the same conclusion—the woman holds a strong hand.

A long, unmoving stare coupled with no threatened call means the woman is simply focusing away from the action in an effort to make the bet seem safe. If you study closely, you'll also see that this player is holding her cards in a gesture slightly indicative of a pass. You must not be mislead by the subtleness of this tell. She is trying to encourage a bet. And the most likely reason a player would want to encourage a bet is because he or she is about to raise.

## BEST STRATEGY:

Don't bet into this player. Don't call without a very strong hand.

*Photo 88:*
*The bet is coming from the man in the checked shirt.*
*His opponent is the woman at right.*

# Discouraging Your Bet

The advantage in knowing when an opponent is trying to *encourage* your bet is this: You can save the money or chips you would have otherwise wagered. That's because most times you won't have a hand big enough to either bet or call against an apparently strong hand. Even if you do have a fairly big hand, you can simply check now and call later. That way, you won't wager first and then be faced with calling a surprise raise.

The advantage in knowing when an opponent is trying to *discourage* your bet is different: You can earn extra money or chips by betting marginal hands in the hope of getting called by hands that are even weaker. There is another great advantage: You can sometimes bluff into the player with a reasonable chance of success. Keep in mind that players holding weaker-than-average hands are less likely to call than players holding hands of unknown strength. Players who are trying to discourage your bet usually have weaker-than-average hands.

One more thing. Just as with the tells relating to players who are trying to encourage your bet, you'll seldom see a tell as blatant as the one in the next photograph. Though the signs may be more subtle, search and you'll find them. But even the *exact* tell photographed will be seen occasionally.

# TELL #45

**TITLE:**

How much do you want to bet, sucker?

**CATEGORY:**

Discouraging Your Bet.

**DESCRIPTION:**

It's seven stud. The woman is looking at the bettor and grabbing for her stack of chips. Both of these mannerisms are important.

**MOTIVATION:**

She is trying to make her opponent change his mind about betting.

**RELIABILITY:**

Weak players = 97%
Average players = 91%
Strong players = 73%

**VALUE PER HOUR:**

$1 limit = $1.02
$10 limit = $7.30
$100 limit = $51.00

**DISCUSSION.**

Study the woman across the table. Among beginning and intermediate players, this is a common method of trying to prevent a bet. The reason players want to stop you from betting is because they hold weak hands with some possibility of winning. In other words, they'd like to see both hands shown down on the table. Then maybe they can salvage the pot. Reaching for chips is intended to show strength and appear threatening. As you now know, players staring at you are less of a threat than those staring away. So here we have a classic example of a woman combining two tells that point in the same direction (looking at the bettor and reaching for her chips). She is probably holding a marginally weak hand. This gives you opportunities to bet hands you would have otherwise checked.

The seven-stud hand in the foreground is an ideal example of a hand you should bet. It's two pair, jacks over sevens. The opponent has a pair of tens on the board and three small hearts. You should know better than to worry about the flush, because if she had it, she would *not* try to discourage your bet. There is some opportunity to bluff here, but be advised that there's a sexist consideration.

You may not like to make generalizations, but within the science of tells generalizations spell profit. Take this one: In general, women who threaten to call are more likely to follow through and *actually* call than men. Men are more apt to remove fingers from their chips and simply throw their cards away. Therefore, when you see the mannerism pictured, you'll have better success bluffing into a man than into a woman.

**BEST STRATEGY:**

Bet marginal hands for value. Consider bluffing, but with caution.

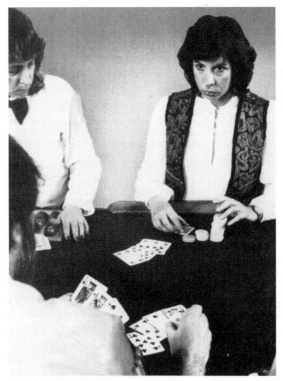

***Photo 89:***
*While the player in the foreground begins to bet, the*
*woman across the table from him stares at him and*
*begins to reach for her chips.*

# Betting Moves

You can often determine the strength of a player's cards just by watching the way he bets. If a player wants a call, he'll be very careful not to frighten you. In his mind, overly forceful or exaggerated betting moves will make his hand appear strong. Bland, timid motions convey weakness, he thinks.

The key to interpreting your opponent's hand by the manner he bets is not very difficult. If the move is too dynamic or exaggerated, you should suspect weakness. If it's quiet and smooth, suspect strength.

When a player couples his wager with the words, "I bet," or something similar in an optimistic or authoritative tone, there's a good chance he's weak or bluffing. If he says nothing or announces his bet in a negative tone, figure him for a strong hand.

In a sense, the whole science of interpreting betting moves runs contrary to what you might at first expect. You've already learned that players who are bluffing or weak often try to blend in with the tablecloth after betting (see *Chapter 5—Tells From Those Who Are Unaware,* Section IV, titled *Nervousness).* Then, shouldn't you expect a player who's bluffing to bet in a very sedate manner so as not to call attention to himself?

No. The reason is that bluffers try to disappear only after their bet. At that time they're not required to do anything but sit and await their fate. While waiting, they try to do nothing that might trigger your call. But while betting, they don't have the luxury of doing nothing. No matter what they might desire, they know they're sure to call attention to themselves while placing the bet. That's why they revert to trying to disguise their hands the only way they know how. They act weak when strong and strong when weak.

Betting with extra emphasis is an attempt to appear strong. It means weak. Betting casually is an attempt to appear weak. It means strong. A casual bet is frequently accompanied by other overt signs of pretended weakness: shrugging, sighing and negative tones of voice.

Sometimes you must be cautious. While a dynamic bet usually means weakness, a few players—particularly sophisticated opponents—will bet with a great deal of force in an attempt to intimidate you into calling. This is how you can tell the difference: A bluff is usually bet with *slightly* or *moderately* force and is generally directed at nobody in particular (or at a player who poses little threat); a strong hand might occasionally be bet with overwhelming force, but that bet will be aimed *specifically* at an opponent who seems to hold a strong hand, and the demeanor of the bettor may well be defiant.

This section is intended as a guide for deciphering the hands of players who *vary* their betting moves. The forthcoming photos will be of little use if you play only against players who use the same betting move all the time.

---

### Caro's Law of Tells #19
*A forceful or exaggerated bet usually means weakness.*

---

### Caro's Law of Tells #20
*A gentle bet usually means strength.*

---

# TELL #46

## TITLE:
Don't let this bet scare you.

## CATEGORY:
Betting Moves.

## DESCRIPTION:
The player gently slides his bet into the pot.

## MOTIVATION:
He's hoping for a call and doesn't want to intimidate his opponent.

## RELIABILITY:
Weak players = 79%
Average players = 71%
Strong players = 63 %

## VALUE PER HOUR:
$1 limit = $0.90
$10 limit = $6.05
$100 limit = $14.00

## DISCUSSION:
Sliding chips is an ideal example of a betting motion chosen by players who hold strong hands and are hoping for calls. Players with weak hands typically feel the need to add extra flair to bolster their bets. This pattern isn't perfect. Occasionally a player may decide to make a timid bluff, but that's rare. If you find such a player, remember his or her move so you can capitalize next time it occurs. Mostly, players who bet softly have the goods. One big

word of caution here. Some players always use the same betting move no matter what. If they always slide their chips in the same way, bluffing or not, then you shouldn't apply this tell.

## BEST STRATEGY:

Don't call without a powerful hand.

***Photo 90:***
*The player (center) begins to bet with his right hand.*

*Photo 91:*
*He continues to push the chips toward the pot.*

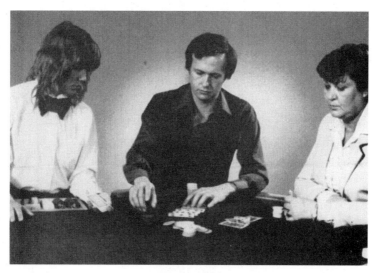

*Photo 92:*
*He completes the bet and casually withdraws his fingers.*

# TELL #47

**TITLE:**

If you call this, you're crazy!

**CATEGORY:**

Betting Moves.

**DESCRIPTION:**

The bettor dances these chips into the pot. Notice his arm reaching far forward. One finger is stiff, indicating that he's attaching a little extra force to the departing chips.

**MOTIVATION:**

He's weak and hopes his bet will be too intimidating to call.

**RELIABILITY:**

Weak players = 98%
Average players = 94%
Strong players = 80%

**VALUE PER HOUR:**

$1 limit = $2.81
$10 limit = $22.65
$100 limit = $183.00

**DISCUSSION:**

Always look for an extended forearm. When you can see almost no bend at the elbow, there's a good chance of a bluff. That happens only rarely, but the action of flinging chips in with a somewhat exaggerated fingertip motion is typical of a bluffer. There's another tell here. The player at right is leaning back and looking at his cards for the first time as the bet is made. If he were leaning forward or paying attention to the bettor, we'd suspect he was acting to prevent a bet by giving the impression he held something powerful. This posture is somewhat different, though, and it makes for a difficult tell. A good theory is that this is genuine indecision. He's probably drawn one card, perhaps to a flush. Now he's squeezing out his hand to see if he made it.

## BEST STRATEGY:

Call this bettor. If you can't win in a showdown, raise.

***Photo 93:***
*Study the bettor (left).*

# TELL #48

**TITLE:**
You've got nothing to worry about, fella.

**CATEGORY:**
Betting Moves.

**DESCRIPTION:**
Compare this photo to Photo 93 of the previous tell. The difference is this: The bettor isn't extending his forearm nearly as far; he's not using his fingertips to emphasize his bet; and he's about to put his chips in gently rather than flinging them.

**MOTIVATION:**
He doesn't want to frighten away the potential caller.

**RELIABILITY:**
Weak players = 91%
Average players = 84 %
Strong players = 70%

**VALUE PER HOUR:**
$1 limit = $1.50
$10 limit = $8.14
$100 limit = $22.00

**DISCUSSION:**
Players who bet gently are likely to hold big hands. In truth, there are occasionally very gentle bets that turn out to be bluffs. In such cases, players are afraid that extra emphasis will lure a call. However, that's rare. By and large, players who bet gently are strong, and you'll make a lot of money

if you consider that the case until they demonstrate otherwise. Also, there's a secondary tell at work. The player at right is doing nothing to discourage this bet. You guessed it! He's ready to pounce, so expect a raise.

## BEST STRATEGY:
Don't call this bet with anything but a respectable hand.

*Photo 94:*
*Here the bettor's arm is not extended as much, and he appears to be placing the chips in more gently.*

# TELL #49

**TITLE:**

Nobody ever called a bet like this and lived to tell about it!

**CATEGORY:**

Betting Moves.

**DESCRIPTION:**

The woman is flinging her bet into the pot.

**MOTIVATION:**

She's weak and wants to appear strong.

**RELIABILITY:**

Weak players = 87 %
Average players = 71%
Strong players = 54%

**VALUE PER HOUR:**

$1 limit = $2.40
$10 limit = $11.00
$100 limit = $44.30

**DISCUSSION:**

Anytime you see a really exaggerated bet, such as the one this woman is making during a seven-stud hand, you should ask yourself this question: Is she betting at anyone in particular? If the answer is yes, there's some chance that she's using the maneuver as a challenge to lure a call. If the answer is no, as it is in this photo, then the betting move is an attempt to show strength and therefore you should suspect that the woman is weak or bluffing.

## BEST STRATEGY:

Call this bet if you have any reasonable hand at all. If you don't, raise as fast as you can—she might pass before you get your chips in!

***Photo 95:***
*This woman is making an exaggerated bet.*

# Tricks

Opponents are always trying to outsmart you. If you're confident that an opponent is acting, remember to ask yourself what he hopes to accomplish. Usually, the answer is astonishingly simple.

Here are two examples of players trying to fool their opponents...

# TELL #50

## TITLE:
You better call quick before I take this pot.

## CATEGORY:
Tricks.

## DESCRIPTION:
The player at left has made a bet. While the opponent at center deliberates, the bettor makes a sweeping gesture to corral the pot. His arms will often remain outstretched until the opponent makes up his mind.

## MOTIVATION:
He's trying to lure a call by using such strange behavior that his opponent will become suspicious.

## RELIABILITY:
Weak players = 64%
Average players = 58%
Strong players = 52%

## VALUE PER HOUR:
$1 limit = $0.07
$10 limit = $0.51
$100 limit = $2.02

## DISCUSSION:
While this may look similar to the tell discussed earlier in Section XIII, *Strong Means Weak* in this chapter (Photo 76), it isn't. In that case the bettor grabbed for the chips while the opponent was passing, acting strong to keep him from reconsidering. Remember, players with winning hands

will give an opponent every opportunity to call. What you see in Photo 96 is a ploy. The opponent hasn't even decided what to do yet. The bettor's hands remain outstretched while he awaits that decision. When you see a pot-snatching mannerism this blatant, you can be pretty sure the bettor wants his actions to appear bizarre. He figures that will earn him a call—and it usually does.

## BEST STRATEGY:

Pass, unless you can beat a solid hand.

*Photo 96:*
*Here's a man reaching for a pot.*

# TELL #51

**TITLE:**

Look! I'm betting no matter what!

**CATEGORY:**

Tricks.

**DESCRIPTION:**

In this sequence, the player seems to look and bet at the same time.

**MOTIVATION:**

He wants his action to appear suspicious enough to lure a call.

**RELIABILITY:**

Weak players = 60%
Average players = 66%
Strong players = 83%

**VALUE PER HOUR:**

$1 limit = $0.13
$10 limit = $1.10
$100 limit = $12.50

**DISCUSSION:**

This is one of those rare tells that works better against strong players than against weak players. Sometimes, particularly in draw poker or seven stud (as shown), you'll meet an opponent who looks at the card or cards he's just caught (here, on seventh street) and prepares to bet at the same time. Many players find it suspicious when they encounter this movement. They feel bewildered and usually call the bet with weak hands. Wrong decision. When a player prepares to bet as he looks at his card, he's usually aware that his action will cause suspicion. In fact, he's using the tactic expressly to encourage a call. Because of that, he'll usually abandon his bet if he doesn't make a winning hand. Also, there's a good chance he *already* has the hand made and is looking and betting at the same time just to lure a call.

## BEST STRATEGY:

Anytime you see a player seem to look at his card while beginning to bet, then complete his bet without hesitation, he's trying to fool you into thinking he would have bet no matter what. You need a very strong hand to call the bet pictured.

*Photo 97:*
*It's seven stud and this player is reaching for his chips as he begins to peek at his seventh and final card.*

*Photo 98:*
*He continues the bet as he picks up the card.*

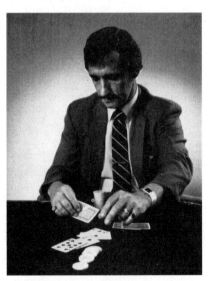

*Photo 99:*
*Smoothly he completes the bet.*

## PLAY BY PLAY:

In the photo, the game is seven-card stud. Increasingly, I see this same tell attempted in hold 'em. This happens when an opposing player is first to act on the river. Your opponent will get ready to bet and then follow through in one fluid motion if the river card connects. If it doesn't, he simply abandons the bet mid-course and checks, instead.

Remember, this type of action is usually a ploy. Your opponent knows that his bet will seem as if it were started prematurely. He thinks this will make you suspicious and more likely to call. In fact, that's the whole idea. He's gambling that he can make you more likely to call. That's good, he figures, *if* he makes the hand.

But if he doesn't make the hand, he won't bluff. That would be silly, because he's already tried to encourage you to call. So, if he misses, he'll check.

Of course, you should also be on the alert for the possibility that your opponent has *already* made a strong hand. But whether he already has it or makes it on the river, if he follows through with his bet, beware.

One more thing. I often take advantage of the times when an opponent abandons this bet. That usually means he's missed the hand. Now I can bet mediocre hands back into him with impunity, not fearing a raise, hoping that he'll make a weak call in an attempt to catch me bluffing.

This MCU Poker Chart deals with hold 'em. You're in seat #1. Your main competitor is in seat #6. Although we never actually get to the showdown, I've displayed his cards face up at the bottom of the chart, so you can verify that the tell was accurate.

## MCU Poker Chart

**Game:** Hold 'em  **Structure:** $25 and $50 blinds, $50 bets on starting hand and flop, $100 thereafter.

| *1* | 2 | 3 | 4 | 5 | 6 | 7 | 8 | 9 | 10 | Pot |
|---|---|---|---|---|---|---|---|---|---|---|
| | | ● | b25 | b50 | | | | | | $75 |
| J♦J / J♠J | | | | | | | | | | **Starting hands** <<< |
| | | | | | ►=50 =100 | =50 =100◄ | — | — | — | $425 |
| ▲100[1] | — | — | — | =100 | | | | | | |
| 50[2] | | | | ►✓ — | ✓ =50 | ✓ —◄ | | | | **Flop** 10♣10 / 2♣2 / A♦A <<< $550 |
| 100[3] | | | | | ►✓ =100◄ | | | | | **Turn** 10♦10 <<< $750 |
| —[5]◄ | | | | | ►=100[4] | | | | | **River** 3♣3 <<< $850 |
| J♦J / J♠J | | | | | 9♣9 / 8♣8 WIN[6] | | | | | **Two-card hands revealed** (no actual show-down) <<< |

---

**Chart key:** Action reads left to right, top to bottom. Each betting round begins ▸ with and ends with ◂ . Other markings and symbols: a (ante); b (blind bet); ✔ (check); = (call); ▲ (raise); – (fold); ● (dealer position, a.k.a. "the button"). A seat number surrounded by asterisks (for example, *1*) is your seat. Any wager not preceded by a symbol is a voluntary first bet. Wagers indicate the total invested on a betting round. The money in the rightmost column indicates total pot size after the betting.

---

## MCU POKER CHART NOTES

*(See corresponding numbers within chart.)*

**1)** You can make an argument for just calling with this pair of jacks. And sometimes I do just call, but rarely. The advantages of just calling, rather than raising, are mostly related to deception. Also, you might be able to fold the hand cheaply if higher cards flop and someone bets—or, especially, if there's a bet and a raise before the action reaches you. But usually you'll want to raise before the flop, because you probably have the best hand, because you might chase away hands with higher cards that could easily beat you, and because you want to take advantage of your late position. So, you raise.

**2)** Everyone checks to you. Had a player bet, say the player in seat #6, the main thing you would fear is an ace. If the opponent has an ace, it might be with a weak kicker, because he didn't raise before the flop. Or he might have a ten. There's also the possibility of a flush draw—and, worse he could have the ace of clubs and another club, giving him a pair of aces *and* the best flush draw. Or he could have flopped three of a kind, two pair—or he could be bluffing. It would be hard to determine. But he didn't bet—nobody did. They all checked.

So, you've got to ask yourself, *how many of those things that we just talked about are still possible?* The answer is that they *all* are! But the theory of correct poker strategy dictates that after players check, their most powerful holdings become *less* likely. Sure, they could be sandbagging, but they *should* sandbag only occasionally, while usually betting with strong hands. Of course, there are some players who do just the opposite. Some almost always sandbag strong hands, waiting for you to bet. But players like that are easy to beat (you simply don't bet weak hands very often after they check) and, anyway, these people aren't that type.

If you usually check this hand because of fear, you're making a mistake. You need to usually have the courage to bet, because there's profit in doing that in the long run. So, you bet $50. Only player #6 calls.

**3)** Again, you should usually bet. Player #6 might be trying for a check-raise, but it's worth the risk. Since he checked but just called on the previous betting round, a check-raise now becomes less likely (although that tactic is a particular favorite of mine). You should worry a little about the possibility of three tens, but you should still bet more than you should check. And you do bet $100.

**4)** THE TELL. The opponent in seat #6 reaches for his chips to begin his betting motion even before the river card...

is turned face up by the dealer. He is staring at the board as his motion continues. As soon as he recognizes the river card, he completes his bet. It all looks like one smooth motion, but wait! This is just the hold 'em variation of the tell we've already discussed. Your opponent has done all this with the intention of making you suspicious of his bet. He is trying to win a call. But he is *only* prepared to complete the bet *if* he makes his flush! Otherwise, he instantly would change this betting movement so that it would appear to be a checking movement.

**5)** Knowing this, you wisely fold after he completes the bet. And, normally, you would have reluctantly called—barring some other tell—because the river card was unlikely to help this player, other than by making a flush. You would usually call—because the size of the pot is much greater than the size of the bet—hoping the opponent were bluffing. Usually you would lose, but you only need to win once in a while to break even. Here you use a powerful tell to save a whole $100 that you would have almost definitely lost without spotting it. In this case, the tell was blatant and even more likely than usual to be accurate.

**6)** And as the cards show, you were right!

# SOME GENERAL TELLS

Here is a collection of tells not specifically covered in the first two parts. You will discover many links between these and the mannerisms previously discussed. Still, each of the next four chapters deals with an important new aspect of tell science. For that reason, the concepts deserve to be studied separately.

# Choosing Your Seat

The seat you select in a poker game can do much to determine how much you'll earn. Many players choose their seats on the basis of hunches or superstition.

When there's a choice of chairs available, you can watch them stand near the table overwhelmed by the decision they must make. They wait, sometimes for ten seconds or more, until the inspiration strikes them. Then their spine tingles mysteriously, a mental arrow points the direction and they approach the lucky seat confidently.

Some people think superstition is silly and a seat's a seat. That's half right. Superstition is silly, but a seat is *not* a seat. Some are much better than others. Not only is seat selection important when you first enter a game, it's often profitable to *change* seats when a better one becomes available. Remember, poker action moves clockwise.

Some of the most valuable reasons for choosing a certain seat are not tell related. It's good to sit behind (to the left) of opponents who play too many pots but who are unaggressive. That way when you raise, these players will already have money invested. If you're on their right and raise, they probably won't play and you'll lose their action. Also, sit to the left of very aggressive, knowledgeable players. They can interfere with your strategy, so let them act first.

In games where there's a forced blind bet, there are two things to consider. First, it's good to be immediately to the right of a player who doesn't defend his blind by calling frequently enough. That way you can bet very weak hands when nobody else has entered the pot and you'll often win his blind and the antes without a fight. Second (and more important), sit to the left of players who are timid in attacking your blind. Since the nature of poker dictates that players in early positions must enter pots more selectively than those in late positions, the last players to act are often left with the opportunity of attacking your blind. If the players immediately to your right are timid, they'll often let you keep your blind and win the antes. That's a bonus for your bankroll.

All those considerations are hard to balance and often it's tough to determine the best seat on a purely strategic basis. Additionally, you may enter a game where you know little or nothing about the habits of the players.

In that case, there's an important tell you should know…

---

### Caro's Law of Tells #21
*When in doubt, sit behind the money.*

---

# TELL #52

## TITLE:
Where is the treasure buried?

## CATEGORY:
Choosing Your Seat.

## DESCRIPTION:
You have just approached this table. It's hold 'em and these opponents seem harmless enough. Should you take the chair in front of you or walk around the table to claim that vacant seat?

## MOTIVATION:
You're trying to pick the most profitable seat.

## RELIABILITY:
Weak players = 62%
Average players = 60%
Strong players = 58%

## VALUE PER HOUR:
$1 limit = $1.00
$10 limit = $9.50
$100 limit = $80.00

## DISCUSSION:
If you take the seat in the foreground, you'll be better off. The key is the man at your right. He has a lot of chips and they're stacked haphazardly. This indicates he will probably be playing loose poker. Remember, you want to sit to the left of players who are loose, so, if you decide to raise, they'll already be in the pot. You certainly don't want

to chase away their action by raising.

If the chips were stacked more neatly, your decision would be the same. You might then figure that this man is winning by skill and you'd just as soon see what he does before you act. In any case, you're about to sit in this game to earn a profit. Because of positional play in poker, you usually have more opportunities to win the money on your right than the money on your left or across the table. That's why, as a general rule, you should position as many chips on your right as possible.

## BEST STRATEGY:

Take one step forward and sit right down.

*Photo 100:*
*Two seats are available. One is right in front of you and the other is at the far end of the table.*

# Conflicting Tells

Tells aren't always as clear as we'd like them to be. On rare occasions, you'll see two or more concurrent mannerisms that seem to suggest different things.

Relax. It's easy to figure out. Often, the opponent is aware of only *some* of his actions. He's acting, but it's not a whole-body act. Therefore, this can be resolved simply by judging which mannerism is most likely to be an act.

If a man seems about to throw his cards away with one very visible gesture while his other hand is slyly creeping toward his chips, the puzzle is resolved. The hand doing the passing is the one he figures you're aware of. His *act is* that he's weak and about to surrender. The other hand is in the background and it's inching toward his chips. If that were an act, he'd make it more blatant—perhaps touching the top of his stacks in a claw-like manner.

The hundreds of common combinations of conflicting tells can't be itemized. When you see a conflict, probably one part of the player is acting and one isn't. The act is whatever he thinks you're aware of. The rest is unconscious.

One type of tell conflict is common and very profitable to observe. Wanna see it?

---

### Caro's Law of Tells #22
*When tells conflict, the player is acting. Determine what he's trying to make you do by his most blatant mannerism. Then generally do the opposite.*

---

# TELL #53

## TITLE:
I don't see you. Honestly, I don't.

## CATEGORY:
Conflicting Tells.

## DESCRIPTION:
Here the man on the right does not want to discourage the bet. He won't look at the bettor directly, but his eyes tell a different story.

## MOTIVATION:
He's hungry for this bet.

## RELIABILITY:
Weak players = 100%
Average players = 94%
Strong players = 85 %

## VALUE PER HOUR:
$1 limit = $3.00
$10 limit = $18.00
$100 limit = $105.00

## DISCUSSION:
Take a good look at the player in the dark shirt. This guy's going to raise. It's seven stud and his three exposed cards are six, nine, seven of mixed suits. In the hole he has an eight and a ten, providing him with a straight. Are you supposed to know that just by looking at the photo? Of course not! I peeked at his hand. What you *do* know is that this man has a very strong combination of cards and is

seeking the bet. His head—that's the part he thinks his opponent may be conscious of—is locked straight ahead and he refuses to pose a threat by turning toward the bettor. But his eyes secretly monitor the action.

### BEST STRATEGY:
Abandon this bet.

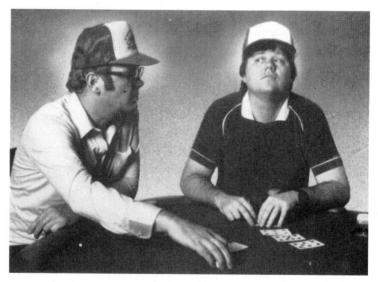

*Photo 101:*
*The player at right is struggling to keep his face pointed away from the bet. But look at his eyes!*

# TELL #54

**TITLE:**
I better not grab too soon.

**CATEGORY:**
Conflicting Tells.

**DESCRIPTION:**
In this case, the woman's eyes are watching the bet. However, that's not what she expects you to be aware of. Her head is turned away and she's practically passing with her left hand.

**MOTIVATION:**
She doesn't want to give the bettor anything to worry about.

**RELIABILITY:**
Weak players = 100%
Average players = 96%
Strong players = 90%

**VALUE PER HOUR:**
$1 limit = $3.05
$10 limit = $24.50
$100 limit = $190.00

**DISCUSSION:**
This common tell leaves no room for doubt. Her head *is* turned away—an act. She *is* acting as if to pass—an act. And her eyes *are* following the bet—*not* an act. Memorize this photo. You're looking at a woman who holds a very strong hand.

## BEST STRATEGY:
Do not bet.

***Photo 102:***
*Here's a more exaggerated version of the previous.*

# Gaining Information

Since tells are very valuable, it's beneficial to encourage them. If you can intimidate your opponents, they'll provide more and easier tells. This is a fact of poker life. Players who remain calm, rational and in control are better able to camouflage their hands.

If you play a powerful, aggressive, winning poker, your opponents will feel threatened. If you can convince them that you are master of your table, they will fight back with ill-conceived efforts designed to confuse you. These actions and reactions will be desperate and primitive: weak when strong, strong when weak. So, just by playing sensible, aggressive poker, you'll invite abundant tells.

Beyond that, there are specific things you can do in special situations to elicit tells. Here are some of them.

# TELL #55

**TITLE:**
A tale with two endings.

**CATEGORY:**
Gaining Information.

**DESCRIPTION:**
It's draw poker, jacks-or-better to open, and in Photo 103 the professional player at center takes three. In response, his opponent (the woman wearing the striped blouse) draws one card. At this point, the pro has made aces up. He would like to bet if the woman has two pair. But if, instead, she was drawing one to a straight or a flush, it would be senseless and dangerous to bet. So, in Photo 105 he pretends to bet and gets a threatening response. Photo 106 is a substitute ending for the same information-gathering maneuver. This time the woman's response is quite different.

**MOTIVATION:**
The professional is trying to gain information about the advisability of a bet.

**RELIABILITY:**
Weak players = 94%*
Average players = 83 %*
Strong players = 64%*

*NOTE: These percentages of reliability apply to the response of the player at which the information-gaining ploy is aimed.*

## VALUE PER HOUR:
$1 limit = $1.69
$10 limit = $13.80
$100 limit = $84.00

## DISCUSSION:
If the pro gets the response shown in Photo 105, he'll go right ahead and bet. The woman is threatening to call, so she's hoping he won't wager. Figure her for two small pair. In Photo 106, the woman looks away with that ubiquitous ready-to-pounce mannerism. She's made a straight, a flush or a full house—take my word for it. For that reason, the expert will check, allow the woman to bet, pretend to ponder, and then pass quietly without losing a single extra chip.

## BEST STRATEGY:
If the rules of your game allow you to fake a bet without completing it, try this maneuver once in a while. Don't overdo it or your opponents will catch on.

*Photo 103:*
*The professional at center draws three cards.*

***Photo 104:***
*His opponent in the striped blouse draws one.*

***Photo 105:***
*The professional reaches for his chips as if to bet and, in response, the woman reaches for her chips threateningly and fans his cards.*

***Photo 106:***
*But the professional might not have been answered with the response in Photo 105. He might have seen this instead.*

# TELL #56

## TITLE:

Let me make sure.

## CATEGORY:

Gaining Information.

## DESCRIPTION:

When the player at left begins to bet, the professional decides to put him under a little pressure. He has no intention of calling so far, but if he gets the right tell... well, that's a different story. So, in the second photo (108), the pro reaches for his chips as if to call. This may look like the same bet-preventing move used by weak and average players, but it isn't. This is a professional ploy designed to yield valuable information. In this case (Photo 109), the pro causes the bettor to double-check his hand. Then (Photo 110), the bet is finally completed with greater-than-average force.

## MOTIVATION:

The pro is planning to pass, but he's hoping to gain information that will save him the pot.

## RELIABILITY:

Weak players = 90%*
Average players = 80%*
Strong players = 61%*

*NOTE: These percentages of reliability apply to the response of the player at which the information-gaining ploy is aimed.

## VALUE PER HOUR:
$1 limit = $3.30
$10 limit = $25.00
$100 limit = $171.00

## DISCUSSION:
This is an extremely valuable maneuver. If the player continues or accelerates his bet in response to the faked calling motion, the pro will "reconsider" for a few seconds and then pass. If, however, the grab for calling chips causes the bettor to look back at his hand, there's an excellent chance that the bet is weak or an outright bluff. If, after some hesitation, the player decides to go through with a bluff, he'll usually bet with extra emphasis as shown. This is an effort to appear strong (which means weak), so the pro will simply call and win the pot. If the player abandons his bet, that's also a big benefit for the pro. He will now win a pot on showdown when he wasn't prepared to call before his maneuver. On a few rare occasions, the player will double-check his hand for legitimate reasons. Then he'll come out betting rather sedately. This lack of force indicates one of the few times that a player who was made to hesitate really *did* have a strong hand. In such a case, the pro will pass.

## BEST STRATEGY:
Use this technique only in the absence of other tells, because its overuse will wise up opponents and diminish the long-range effectiveness.

*Photo 107:*
*The player at left is betting.*

*Photo 108:*
*In an effort to gain information, the expert at center*
*reaches for his chips.*

***Photo 109:***
*This causes the bettor to take a second look at his cards.*

***Photo 110:***
*Now he completes the bet forcefully.*

# TELL #57

## TITLE:
You don't scare me.

## CATEGORY:
Gaining Information.

## DESCRIPTION:
Study the previous tell. This is the same maneuver, but the result is different. The bettor does not double-check his hand. Instead, he completes his bet with absolutely no hesitation.

## MOTIVATION:
The pro is seeking to learn if the bettor is truly strong.

## RELIABILITY:
Weak players = 90%*
Average players = 83 %*
Strong players = 57%*

*NOTE: These percentages of reliability apply to the response of the player at which the information-gaining ploy is aimed.*

## VALUE PER HOUR:
$1 limit = $0.47
$10 limit = $3.50
$100 limit = $17.00

## DISCUSSION:
The only difference between this and the tell we just studied is that the player isn't intimidated. The pro fails to make the opponent hesitate. This usually indicates strength, so passing is in order. Also notice that the bettor places his

chips softly into the pot so as not to appear too strong. He really wants this call, but he's destined to be disappointed.

## BEST STRATEGY:

This is the same maneuver as discussed in the previous tell. Remember not to overuse this strategy.

***Photo 111:***
*The player at left begins to bet.*

***Photo 112:***
*The expert at center is using the same maneuver as in the previous tell.*

***Photo 113:***
*This time the player completes his bet without hesitation.*

# Misdirected Bets

Any bet that challenges a secondary contender is a dead giveaway. It almost always means weakness.

If you had a strong hand, would you go out of your way to bet in a manner designed to challenge the player who was *least* likely to call? Of course not! If you wanted to challenge somebody, you'd go straight after the guy who's got a hand powerful enough to pay you off. That's simple sense. Bettors who violate that logic (by aiming their wager at or focusing their attention on someone who's scarcely a threat) are not having mental lapses. They are doing this by design, to make the strong hand feel that he is not even the real threat.

Don't you be fooled. When they bet, players with winning hands pay attention to their strongest-appearing opponents. If the most likely challenger is being ignored by the bettor, that's a bluff. Period.

It's too bad this kind of tell doesn't occur frequently; then it would be worth a great deal more money.

> *Caro's Law of Tells #23*
> *A misdirected bet is almost always a bluff.*

# TELL #58

## TITLE:

Why should aces scare me when I can beat this guy over here?

## CATEGORY:

Misdirected Bets.

## DESCRIPTION:

It seems like the player at left is going to a lot of trouble to bet past the man with these cards showing...

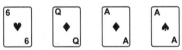

He's reaching clear across the table to challenge this...

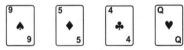

Does that make sense to you?

## MOTIVATION:

An attempt to make the stronger opponent feel insignificant in this pot.

## RELIABILITY:

Weak players = 92%
Average players = 87%
Strong players = 84 %

## VALUE PER HOUR:

$1 limit = $0.65
$10 limit = $4.04
$100 limit = $22.80

## DISCUSSION:

It seems reasonable that the man's hand at right contains garbage—possibly a failed straight. Ask yourself why the player would be reaching way across the table and betting into the weaker-looking of his two opponents. The answer is not very involved. This guy's bluffing. He probably holds something like a pair of kings.

Look at the expression of the man in the middle. He's thinking, and rightly so, "Hey, what about me? I'm in this pot, too!" Suppose you were the bettor and you wanted to be called. Say you had a hidden full house. Would you reach halfway to Cleveland to threaten a player who doesn't figure to call? Well, neither would this guy.

## BEST STRATEGY:

Call as quickly as your fingers will allow.

***Photo 114:***
*This is seven stud. The player wearing the hat has a pair of aces showing, but the player on the right has truly ugly cards. So why is this bet being directed across the table?*

# THE SOUNDS OF TELLS

A long-time poker professional once said he could beat anyone at poker with his eyes closed. What he meant was that his opponents told him the strength of their hands just by the sounds they made.

He was not aware of the similar work I'd done which a gambling magazine had already published. When we compared notes, a few of his conclusions were the same as mine. However, he'd gone about his research in a very cumbersome fashion. Instead of using the basic tools of tell science—*weak means strong* and *strong means weak*—he had catalogued the things that people said and tried to uncover trends. He claimed that most of the things he heard had very little relevance to whether or not they were bluffing. But if they asked "How much is it to me?" and then raised, you could be pretty sure that they weren't bluffing.

That was a good conclusion. Players who ask for *any* clarification of the rules before they raise are legitimately strong. Often they already *know* the answer to their questions. By acting dumb, they're trying to convey that they're uncertain—that perhaps they'll raise or bet only if it doesn't cost too much. This is an *act* to appear weak and unsure. You should seldom call when a player asks, "How much is it to raise?"

Generally, it isn't the words your opponents choose as much as their tone of voice that gives you clues as to the strength of their hands. Anytime a player uses a sad tone, he or she is trying to feign weakness. Remember, pretended weakness means strength, so you should be cautious about calling sad tones. Especially cheerful tones are attempts to show contentment. Usually, these mean weakness.

Do you see how the sounds of tells follow the great principles of all other tell sciences? If a player is *acting,* whether it's by gesture or by voice, you should usually be persuaded to respond in a manner *opposite* of what he's trying to make you do.

If your opponent sounds threatening, figure him to be weak. If he sounds uncertain, figure him to be strong. If he sounds as if betting is misery, pass. If he chirps the words "I bet," as if his hand obviously merits a bet, call.

One of the great clues is the standard everyday sigh. When you hear an opponent sigh, he's trying to make you think he's disappointed. He isn't! Players sigh only if they hold strong hands. Any player who accompanies his bet with a sigh is performing the equivalent of shrugging his shoulders. In fact, you may encounter both the sigh and the shrug on the same wager. Both are intended to imply weakness or uncertainty. Both, in fact, mean strength and should seldom be called.

Often a player will sigh even before it's time to bet. This may happen when, for instance, he looks at the cards he's just drawn or sees the flop. Listen for that sigh, and when you hear it, beware.

Sometimes you'll meet a player who hums or whistles, usually quietly to himself or herself. This is *not* an act. Some players like to pass the time between hands in this manner. If the humming or whistling stops suddenly, you can be pretty sure the player just looked at a strong hand

and intends to play. He is now concentrating.

The same is true of people who chatter continuously. When they are dealt a strong hand and intend to play, they must concentrate. At that time, their chatter will either cease or become erratic.

Keeping all this in mind, let's deal with one very important tell sound.

Do me a favor. Put your tongue on the inside edge of your teeth at the top of your mouth. Create some suction. Now withdraw your tongue briskly.

Did you hear that sound? Do it again. Again. Once more. Again.

I want you to remember that sound. It's a clack. I'm not sure that's a good definition, but it will have to do. No, on second thought, it *won't* have to do. Let's call it *Pokerclack* and that way we'll always know what we mean.

You'll hear Pokerclack fairly often in a game. Whenever you do, you must throw away any less-than-monster hand just as quickly as you are able. That's because you're usually going to hear this sound coming from an opponent who has an almost certain winner.

Remember, most weak to medium players tend to act weak when they're strong. That's why it's usually bad policy to call a player who goes out of his way to sigh, shrug or act sad in any way.

Well, Pokerclack is a sad sound. Just to prove it, do this. Get ready to make Pokerclack. Put your tongue in the right position and apply suction.

Do not release Pokerclack.

Are you following instructions? Now suppose a friend walks up to you and says, "I just lost my whole month's pay at roulette."

Release Pokerclack now.

Aha! It sounded right, didn't it? It was an audible

display of negativeness. Your friend would have interpreted it as such. As if you had said, "That's really too bad!"

But we know from previous tells that if a player goes out of his way to convey sorrow, he's probably got a winner. Therefore, a player making this sound at poker does *not* hold a bad hand.

---

*Caro's Law of Tells #24*
*Beware of sighs and sounds of sorrow.*

---

*Caro's Law of Tells #25*
*Don't call Pokerclack.*

---

# IMPORTANT TELLS
# REVISITED

Now we're going to take another look at some important tells. You should use this section to refresh your memory and, perhaps, gain new insights before taking your final exam.

### Photo 115:
*Remember that players who stack their chips neatly are apt to play conservatively. The messy chips to the side are likely to represent this man's profit. He may play more liberally with those.*

### Photo 116:
*Again, expect this woman to play conservatively because her chips are neatly stacked. There's another tell at work here. It's seven stud and she's chosen to adjust her first three cards in an orderly fashion. If she's an experienced player, that probably doesn't mean much. But if she's a beginner, it probably hints that she's interested in playing this hand.*

***Photo 117:***
*This player has bet and now decides to share his hand with a friend who's standing behind him, It's unlikely that he's bluffing.*

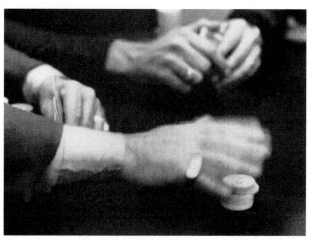

***Photo 118:***
*Don't call that shaking hand. It's seldom a bluff.*

**Photo 119:**
*Here's one of the most valuable tells in poker. First, the woman looks at her final card in seven stud...*

**Photo 120:**
*Now she instantly and automatically glances at her chips. This means she likes her hand and intends to bet.*

**Photo 121:**
*Quickly she looks away from her chips. If you were looking at your own hand when she glanced at her chips, you would have missed this profitable tell.*

***Photo 122:***
*Let's take another look at the glance-at-chips tell.*
*This time it's draw poker and the player at right is*
*asking for three cards.*

***Photo 123:***
*He picks up his three replacements, looks at them, and...*

***Photo 124:***
*Now he looks immediately at his chips. The glance*
*generally lasts less than a second, so if you're not*
*watching your opponent, you miss it. When you see an*
*opponent glance at his chips, you can be fairly sure he*
*likes his hand and intends to bet.*

***Photo 125:***
*This is draw poker. The woman picks up the first three
cards that have been dealt to her...*

***Photo 126:***
*She has securely transferred these to her left hand. Now
she picks up the rest of her cards...*

***Photo 127:***
*She guards these and looks away from the
action. Whenever you see a player guard cards,
and then look away as if uninterested, you should
expect a bet or a raise.*

*Photo 128:*
*The woman is conspicuously looking away from the bettor and acting almost as if to pass. That combination usually means a raise is coming.*

*Photo 129:*
*It's hold 'em and this woman watches the flop.*

*Photo 130:*
*Seconds later she continues to study. This usually shows weakness, particularly among players who habitually look away when the flop pleases them.*

***Photo 131:***
*This draw poker player picks up
two aces and a king—a pretty
powerful beginning...*

***Photo 132:***
*Now he's secured these in his
left hand, and adds two dream
cards, an ace and a king, giving him
aces full...*

***Photo 133:***
*Immediately he puts these two new
cards with his first three...*

***Photo 134:***
*And now he guards the whole hand.
This tell can be contrasted to the
common habit of continuing to
stare at weak cards.*

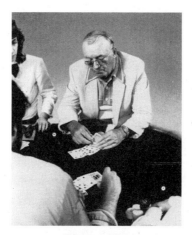

***Photo 135:***
*The player in the foreground is beginning to bet a marginal seven stud hand. Judging by the player across the table, the wager is safe. When players stare at their cards in response to a coming bet, they're trying to discourage the bet. If this man held a strong hand, why would he want to prevent your bet?*

***Photo 136:***
*Compare this to the previous photo. The man in the foreground is again about to bet a marginal hand. This time his opponent looks away and pretends to be passing prematurely. This is always dangerous. Expect a raise.*

***Photo 137:***
*Here's another way a player might try to prevent the man in the foreground from betting. The man is staring at the bettor and reaching for his chips in a threatening manner. Remember, players who try to prevent your bets are weak and you should not be afraid to wager with medium-strong hands.*

***Photo 138:***
*Any exaggerated betting move is likely to be a bluff. Here we see an unnaturally raised forearm.*

***Photo 139:***
*If the head is turned away from the action, but the eyes are watching, beware. Don't be surprised if this man raises.*

### *Photo 140:*
*Sometimes you can determine whether or not an opponent is bluffing just by reaching for your chips. That's what the player is doing in the foreground as this woman bets. In response, she shows no hesitation as she hurries to complete the bet. This means she has a strong hand.*

### *Photo 141:*
*Take another look at the previous photo and compare it to this one. Here, again, the player in the foreground reaches for his chips as the woman wagers. This time she hesitates and looks back at her hand. If she completes the bet, particularly with extra force, there's a great chance that she's bluffing.*

***Photo 142:***
*The seven stud player at center has just received a third
card up and now he peeks at his hole cards. Always ask
yourself why an opponent would be double-checking.
Often players know the ranks of their hole cards but not
their suits. If, for instance, an opponent's board shows
three suited cards and he checks his hole cards, he's
searching for one more of that suit to provide a flush
opportunity. He'd seldom have a flush already
completed. It's unlikely that he'd need to double check if
he held two of the matching suit in the hole (although
some players do double-check just in case their memory
is tricking them). After a player who just caught a third
suited card peeks in the hole, you should be less worried
about his already-made flush.*

***Photo 143:***
*The seven stud player at center is deliberately positioning his bet to challenge a player who doesn't seem to be a threat. He's ignoring the woman with a pair of kings showing. Anytime a player misdirects a bet into a player who does not pose an apparent threat, you should suspect a bluff.*

# CARO'S LAWS OF TELLS: A SUMMARY

Here is a listing of all the Caro's Laws of Tells featured in this book. This convenient summary will serve as a quick reference guide to the general ideas involved in the tells you've just learned.

> ### Caro's Great Law of Tells
> *Players are either acting or they aren't. If they are acting, then decide what they want you to do and disappoint them.*

> ### Caro's Law of Tells #1
> *Players often stack chips in a manner directly indicative of their style of play. Conservative means conservative; sloppy means sloppy.*

> ### Caro's Law of Tells #2
> *Players often buy chips in a manner directly indicative of their style of play. Flamboyant means flamboyant; guarded means guarded.*

### Caro's Law of Tells #3
*Any unsophisticated player who bets, then shares his hand while awaiting a call, is unlikely to be bluffing.*

### Caro's Law of Tells #4
*A trembling bet is a force to be feared.*

### Caro's Law of Tells #5
*In the absence of indications to the contrary, call any bettor whose hand covers his mouth.*

### Caro's Law of Tells #6
*A genuine smile usually means a genuine hand; a forced smile is a bluff.*

### Caro's Law of Tells #7
*The friendlier a bettor is, the more apt he is to be bluffing.*

### Caro's Law of Tells #8
*A player glances secretly at his chips only when he's considering a bet—and almost always because he's helped his hand.*

### Caro's Law of Tells #9
*If a player looks and then checks instantly, it's unlikely that he improved his hand.*

### Caro's Law of Tells #10
*If a player looks and then bets instantly, it's unlikely that he's bluffing.*

### Caro's Law of Tells #11

*Disappoint any player who, by acting weak, is seeking your call.*

### Caro's Law of Tells #12

*Disappoint any player who, by acting strong, is hoping you'll pass.*

### Caro's Law of Tells #13

*Players staring at you are usually less of a threat than players staring away.*

### Caro's Law of Tells #14

*Players staring at their cards are usually weak.*

### Caro's Law of Tells #15

*Players reaching for their chips out of turn are usually weak.*

### Caro's Law of Tells #16

*A weak player who gathers a pot prematurely is usually bluffing.*

### Caro's Law of Tells #17

*When a player acts to spread his hand prematurely, it's usually because he's bluffing.*

### Caro's Law of Tells #18

*If a player bets and then looks back at his hand as you reach for your chips, he's probably bluffing.*

> ### Caro's Law of Tells #19
> *A forceful or exaggerated bet usually means weakness.*

> ### Caro's Law of Tells #20
> *A gentle bet usually means strength.*

> ### Caro's Law of Tells #21
> *When in doubt, sit behind the money.*

> ### Caro's Law of Tells #22
> *When tells conflict, the player is acting. Determine what he's trying to make you do by his most blatant mannerism. Then generally do the opposite.*

> ### Caro's Law of Tells #23
> *A misdirected bet is almost always a bluff.*

> ### Caro's Law of Tells #24
> *Beware of sighs and sounds of sorrow.*

> ### Caro's It of Tells #25
> *Don't call Pokerclack.*

# PLAY ALONG
# PHOTO QUIZ

Let's test what you've learned about tells. You'll find the answers at the end of this chapter, along with the chapters you should study if you made any mistakes.

Get ready, get nervous, go...

***Photo 144:***
**Question 1:** *Judging by the way the player at left is taking his money from his wallet, do you expect him to play conservatively or liberally?*

***Photo 145:***
*The seven stud player at left is receiving his final card face down from the dealer...*

*Photo 146:*
*Now he peeks at the card...*

*Photo 147:*
*This is his immediate reaction...*

*Photo 148:*
*...followed by this.* **Question 2:** *Would you bet a me-dium-strength hand into the player at left?*

***Photo 149:***
**Question 3:** *Is the bettor at center bluffing?*

***Photo 150:***
*You're the player in the left foreground. It's seven stud, all the cards have been dealt, and you have two pair, jacks over sevens. Your opponent has a pair of tens on the board and three hearts. She checked before looking at her seventh card, but she knows what it is.*
**Question 4:** *Should you bet or check?*

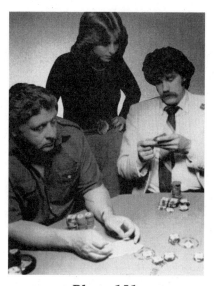

*Photo 151:*
*It's draw poker, after the draw. The player in*
*the suit drew three cards and bet into you.*
*You have two small pair.*
**Question 5:** *Should you call, raise, or pass?*

---

*Photo 152:*
*The man standing is entering the game and*
*buying chips.* **Question 6:** *Do you expect him to play*
*conservatively or aggressively?*

*Photo 153:*
*It's seven stud, six cards have been dealt, and there's just one to come. The woman (center) has three hearts showing and is betting into the woman at right, who we'll say has only one pair.* **Question 7:** *If you were the woman at right, would you call this bet?*

*Photo 154:*
*It's seven stud after all cards have been dealt. Your opponent is looking at his final card. He has four parts of a straight on the board.*

*Photo 155:*
*He is now aware of what his final card is.*

*Photo 156:*
*You have queens up and check.* **Question 8:** *If this man bets, what should you do?*

***Photo 157:***
*It's draw poker. The player second from right has opened
in an early position and now requests three cards.*

***Photo 158:***
*In response, his opponent (far right) asks for one card.*

***Photo 159:***
**Question 9:** *Study the player (right). Is he more likely to
be drawing to a flush or holding a two pair?*

*Photo 160:*
*It's draw poker, jacks or better to open. The player*
*second from left has opened and is taking three cards.*

*Photo 161:*
**Question 10:** *Would you bet jacks up after*
*he checked to you?*

***Photo 162:***
*It's five card draw lowball. The man at left just decided
to draw one card this very second. He had to make his
decision while studying the frozen mannerisms of the
player to his left.* **Question 11:** *How many cards will
that player (second from left) probably draw?*

***Photo 163:***
*It's draw poker, jacks or better to open. The player at left
has called the opener and is taking two cards.*
**Question 12:** *What is the player more likely to have, a
pair of sixes with a high kicker or three sixes?*

***Photo 164:***
*Suppose you're in the left foreground with three aces. It's draw poker and it's your turn to act.*
**Question 13:** *Should you open, or is there another player who will bet for you?*

***Photo 165:***
*It's draw poker and the woman is trying to decide how many to draw.*

***Photo 166:***
*She needed two cards and now she looks at them...*

***Photo 167:***
**Question 14:** *Did the woman help her hand?*

*Photo 168:*
*Suppose you're playing seven stud and are seated to this*
*player's right. You have aces up and are considering a*
*bet.* **Question 15:** *Would your bet be safe?*

*Photo 169:*
*The seven stud player at left is making a bet.*
**Question 16:** *Is the bet safe?*

***Photo 170:***
**Question 17:** *Should you feel safe betting a medium strong hand into this woman?*

---

***Photo 171:***
*The hold 'em player at left watches the flop.*

***Photo 172:***
**Question 18:** *Did this player like the flop?*

*Photo 173:*
**Question 19:** *Would you expect this player's basic game to be liberal or conservative?* Question 20: *Is he presently winning or losing?*

*Photo 174:*
*The player at right is beginning to bet.*
**Question 21:** *Is the player at left going to pass?*

***Photo 175:***
*It's after the draw. The player third from right opened and stood pat. He is now considering whether to bet his king-high straight. The woman in the black sweater called and drew one.*
**Question 22:** *Should the man check or bet?*

***Photo 176:***
*You can choose the seat in the foreground or the one at the end of the table.*
**Question 23:** *Which is better?*

# Photo Quiz Answers

**Question 1:** Conservatively. (Study Section I, *Noncombat Tells*).

**Question 2:** No, you shouldn't bet a medium-strength hand. (Study Section VII, *Glancing at Chips,* and Section XVI, *Encouraging Your Bet.*)

**Question 3:** No, the shrugging bettor is not bluffing. (Study Section XII, *Weak Means Strong.*)

**Question 4:** You should check. The woman is looking away and pretending to pass. (Study Section XVI, *Encouraging Your Bet.*)

**Question 5**: You should pass. (Study Section II, *Sharing a Hand.*)

**Question 6:** The flamboyant manner in which he's buying his chips suggests he'll play aggressively. (Study Section I, *Noncombat Tells.*)

**Question 7:** Yes, you should call this exaggerated bet. (Study Section XVIII, *Betting Moves.*)

**Question 8:** Pass. The opponent told you he made his hand when he looked briefly at his chips. (Study Section VII, *Glancing at Chips.*)

**Question 9:** He's more likely to be holding two pair. (Study Section X, *Instant Reaction.*)

**Question 10:** Yes, you should bet jacks up. The player looked at three cards and checked instantly. (Study Section X, *Instant Reaction.*)

**Question 11:** None. Players who act as if to draw cards out of turn frequently intend to "reconsider" and rap pat. (Study Section XII, *Weak Means Strong.*)

The following photo was taken immediately *after* the one used in this test question.

***Photo 177:***
*The player second from left changes his mind and decides to rap pat. Also see Photo 162 to review what happened before this took place.*

**Question 12:** A pair of sixes with a high kicker. (Study Section XIV, *Exposing Cards.*)

**Question 13:** Don't open. The man in the sweater (third from right) will do it for you. (Study Section XV, *Opening Tells.*)

**Question 14:** No, she didn't help her hand. She's reaching for her chips threateningly. (Study Section XIII, *Strong*

*Means Weak,* Section XVII, *Discouraging Your Bet.*)

**Question 15:** No. The bet is dangerous. (Study Section XXI, *Conflicting Tells*.)

**Question 16:** No. The bet is dangerous. The player at right is looking away and *acting* uninterested. (Study Section XII, *Weak Means Strong*.)

**Question 17:** No! Your bet is very dangerous. You must learn to recognize this tell. It is one of the most profitable and reliable in poker. (Study Section XII, *Weak Means Strong*, and Section XVI, *Encouraging Your Bet*.)

**Question 18:** Yes, he liked the flop. He's looking away as if uninterested. (Study Section XII, *Weak Means Strong*.)

**Question 19:** Basically conservative. His main stacks of chips are neat. (Study Section I, *Noncombat Tells*.)

**Question 20:** He's presently winning. The messy chips are his profits. (Study Section I, *Noncombat Tells*.)

**Question 21:** Probably not. He's acting as if to throw his up card away, but he'll probably only readjust it. (Study Section XII, *Weak Means Strong*.)

**Question 22:** He should check. The woman is looking away. (Study Section XII, *Weak Means Strong*, and Section XVI, *Encouraging Your Bet*.)

**Question 23:** The seat across the table is better. (Study Section XX, *Choosing Your Seat*.)

# FINAL THOUGHTS

### A FINAL TIP

When you spot a tell, you should not act on it instantly! Wait a short time and seem in doubt. That way, your opponent will be less likely to adjust his behavior, and you probably will be able to use that same tell again for more profit.

One of the great mistakes is letting your ego get in the way of your tells. Sometimes you feel so good about spotting a tell that you want to let everyone know how smart you are. Fight this temptation.

I've heard players say something like, "I knew you were bluffing, because you always hold your breath." That may make you feel superior for a minute, but it will also cost you money. It will make your opponent aware of the tell.

My advice is to keep your tell-spotting abilities to yourself. The less players know that you're even aware of this major poker secret, the better off you'll be. Let's keep it just between us.

### A FINAL QUESTION

That brings us back to where we started. In order for you to graduate from this course and advance to the real-world poker tables where the big profit is waiting, you need to answer this one final question. Don't get nervous. Take your time...

***Photo 178:***
**Last Question:** *Would you feel safer betting into a player who looks like this...*

***Photo 179:***
*...or a player who looks like this?*

If you don't know the answer to the final question,
further study is suggested. I recommend
*Mike Caro's Book of Poker Tells.*

# Acknowledgements

For lending their expertise: Doyle Brunson, Bobby Baldwin, Tom McEvoy, Jack Straus, Michael Wiesenberg, John Fox, Victor Resnick, Steve Margulies and particularly Rick Greider.

For technical support and advice: Stanley Sludikoff, Len Miller, Tom Bowling, Arnold Abrams, Jerrold lkazdoy and Steve Steinkamp.

For photography: Cliff Stanley, Lee McDonald, Frank Mitrapi, Raiko Hartman and Allen Photographers of Las Vegas.

For other important contributions: Chip Johnson, Rosemary Dufault, Eloise Nudelman, Arthur Sathmary, Mason Malmuth, David Sklansky and Jerry Weinstein.

Most of those people offered direct contributions, while some (particularly Jack Straus, Bobby Baldwin and David Sklansky) gave useful information in the course of our conversations.

And especially I'd like to thank Phyllis Caro, who insisted that this work be finished without further delay and then made it happen.

Here is a complete list of the *Book of Tells* cast. Most stars appear more than once. The photograph referred to in the "Photo Number" column is one place where the model can be seen. Thanks to all.

| Star | Photo Number |
|---|---|
| Lori Ackerman | 128 (right) |
| Bertha Allen | 32 |
| Melvyn Azaria | 62 |
| Daniel M. Barber | 51 (center) |
| Lynn Beyers | 142 (left) |
| Elba Bogart | 25 (left) |
| Norman J. Bogart | 48 (right) |
| Tom Bowling | 15 (right) |
| Jan Bowman | 102 (left) |
| Mike Boyle | 10 |
| Phyllis Caro | 89 |
| Shelley Carr | 80 (right) |
| Bernard H. Chamberlin | 137 |
| Ed Clemente | 149 (center) |
| Robert Cook | 5 |
| Robert Dennis | 85 (center) |
| Rosemary DuFault | 11 (second from left) |
| Mary F. Eversole | 55 |
| Richard A. Eyler | 3 |
| Edmund Fakhre | 52 (center) |
| Ron Faltinsky | 122 (left) |
| Scott Fawaz | 94 (left) |
| June Field | 30 (right) |
| Charles P. Flater | 8 |
| Steve Flowers | 11 (center) |
| John Fox | 12 (center, seated) |
| Don Galbreth | 25 (center) |
| Phillip Goatz | 69 (left) |
| Dianne Gravalese | 102 (right) |
| Richard Green | 105 (center) |
| Rick Greider | 18 (center) |
| David Heyden | 93 (right) |
| Stuart M. Jacobs | 60 (left) |
| Louis Jannuzzi | 61 |
| Chip Johnson | 122 (right) |
| Charles E. Knight | 135 |
| Audrey Kwasney | 116 |
| Don Maedgen | 18 (right) |
| Paul Mason | 87 |
| Steve McClenahan | 117 |
| Robert Meissner | 101 (left) |
| LeRoy B. Merillat | 142 (right) |

| | |
|---|---|
| Robert A. Miller | 114 (right) |
| Les Mindus | 77 (center) |
| Frank Neuhauser | 6 |
| Ray Noren | 36 (second from right) |
| Helen Saenz | 119 |
| Arlyne Salomon | 77 (second from left) |
| Mina Salomon | 85 (left of center) |
| James A. Salvatore | 152 (standing) |
| Josephine Sathmary | 107 |
| Steve Schlemmer | 19 (center) |
| Roy B. Seider | 19 (right) |
| Tex Sheahan | 86 (center) |
| Joe Shearer | 17 (left) |
| Martha Shirley | 28 (left) |
| Bobbie Lea Stember | 19 (left) |
| John Sutton | 115 |
| Colleen Tarbert | 12 (standing) |
| Jerry Wood | 9 |
| M. Alison Wright | 117 (left) |

*(Note: All the following comments are from the original version of this book. Some of my favorite people listed have sadly died or faded from public view.)*

Among the Tell Stars are more than two dozen world-class players, notably Chip Johnson (famous poker theorist and teacher), Rick Greider (the world's foremost seven-stud expert), John Fox (author of the best-selling *Play Poker, Quit Work, and Sleep Till Noon* and other books), Ron Faltinsky, Richard Green, Ray Noren (an authority on protecting players against cheaters), and David Heyden.

Additionally, there are four managers of major Las Vegas poker rooms: Steve Schlemmer (Palace Station, where many of the photographs were taken), Jan Bowman (Sam's Town), Don Maedgen (Four Queens), and John Sutton (Imperial Palace). Also modeling is Tom Bowling, who was formerly manager of the Palace Station poker room (then called the Bingo Palace) and is now both head of the sports book and Director of Casino Marketing.

Among the major poker journalists pictured are Tex Sheahan, Stuart M. Jacobs, and Norman J. Bogart. LeRoy B. Merillat runs LeRoy's Sports Book in Las Vegas.

More than half the photos were taken at the Palace Station. A special thanks goes to the entire staff of that progressive poker room for its important contribution to the young science of tells. Many of the tells were staged at the Rainbow Club in Gardena, California, which suspended operations in 1983.

The Rainbow was among my favorite places to play, and its closing saddenned me. One other sad thing before we get on with the happy magic of tells: Most of the photographs taken at the studios of Allen Photographers in Las Vegas were lost when that establishment was destroyed by fire in 1983. Only 12 photos survived out of more than 100. Fortunately, everyone who posed at the studios appears in this book. Those lost tells were later reshot at the Palace Station.

The photographs that appear in this book are credited as follows:

**Photographer:** Allen Photographers **Photos:** 18, 93, 94, 114, 117, 128, 149, 152, 173 **Photographer:** Cliff Stanley **Photos:** 86, 102, 115, 131, 132, 133, 134 **Photographer:** Frank Mirani **Photos:** 9, 10, 15, 16, 17, 19, 20, 21, 22, 25, 26, 27, 31, 32, 33, 43, 44, 45, 46, 48, 49, 50, 55, 56. 69, 70, 101, 116, 118, 129, 130, 139, 142, 145, 146, 147, 148, 162, 168, 171, 172, 174, 177 **Photographer:** Lee McDonald **Photos:** 1, 2, 3, 4, 8, 28, 29, 30, 57, 58, 59, 60, 61, 62, 63, 64, 65, 66, 67, 68, 80, 81, 82, 87, 89, 90, 91, 92, 95, 97, 98, 99, 100, 119, 120, 121, 135, 136, 137, 138, 140, 141, 150, 153, 154, 155, 156, 170, 176, 178, 179 **Photographer:** Raiko Hartman **Photos:** 5, 6, 7, 11, 12, 13, 14, 23, 24, 34, 35, 36, 37, 38, 39, 40, 41, 42, 47, 51, 52, 53, 54, 71, 72, 73, 74, 75, 76, 77, 78, 79, 83, 84, 85, 88, 96, 103, 104, 105, 106, 107, 108, 109, 110, 111, 112, 113, 125, 126, 127, 143, 144, 151, 157, 158, 159, 160, 161, 163, 164, 165, 166, 167, 175 **Photos by Amateur** 122, 123, 124, 169

# GRI'S PROFESSIONAL VIDEO POKER STRATEGY
## Win Money at Video Poker! With the Odds!

At last, for the **first time**, and for **serious players only**, the GRI **Professional Video Poker** strategy is released so you too can play to win! **You read it right** - this strategy gives you the **mathematical advantage** over the casino and what's more, it's **easy to learn!**

**PROFESSIONAL STRATEGY SHOWS YOU HOW TO WIN WITH THE ODDS** - This **powerhouse strategy**, played for **big profits** by an **exclusive** circle of **professionals**, people who make their living at the machines, is now made available to you! You too can win - with the odds - and this **winning strategy** shows you how!

**HOW TO PLAY FOR A PROFIT** - You'll learn the **key factors** to play on a **pro level**: which machines will turn you a profit, break-even and win rates, hands per hour and average win per hour charts, time value, team play and more! You'll also learn big play strategy, alternate jackpot play, high and low jackpot play and key strategies to follow.

**WINNING STRATEGIES FOR ALL MACHINES** - This **comprehensive, advanced pro package** not only shows you how to win money at the 8-5 progressives, but also, the **winning strategies** for 10s or better, deuces wild, joker's wild, flat-top, progressive and special options features.

**BE A WINNER IN JUST ONE DAY** - In just one day, after learning our strategy, you will have the skills to **consistently win money** at video poker - with the odds. The strategies are easy to use under practical casino conditions.

**FREE BONUS - PROFESSIONAL PROFIT EXPECTANCY FORMULA ($15 VALUE)** - For serious players, we're including this free bonus essay which explains the professional profit expectancy principles of video poker and how to relate them to real dollars and cents in your game.

# GREAT POKER BOOKS
## ADD THESE TO YOUR LIBRARY - ORDER NOW!

**TOURNAMENT POKER** *by Tom McEvoy* - Rated by pros as best book on tournaments ever written, and enthusiastically endorsed by more than 5 world champions, this is a *must* for every player's library. Packed solid with winning strategies for all 11 games in the *World Series of Poker*, with extensive discussions of 7-card stud, limit hold'em, pot and no-limit hold'em, Omaha high-low, re-buy, half-half tournaments, satellites, strategies for each stage of tournaments. Big player profiles. 344 pages, paperback, $39.95.

**OMAHA HI-LO POKER** *by Shane Smith* - Learn essential winning strategies for beating Omaha high-low; the best starting hands, how to play the flop, turn, and river, how to read the board for both high and low, dangerous draws, plus powerful chapter on winning low-limit tournaments. Smith shows the differences between Omaha high-low and hold'em strategies. Includes odds charts, glossary, low-limit tips, strategic ideas. 84 pages, 8 x 11, spiral bound, $17.95.

**7-CARD STUD (THE COMPLETE COURSE IN WINNING AT MEDIUM & LOWER LIM-ITS)** *by Roy West* - Learn the latest strategies for winning at $1-$4 spread-limit up to $10-$20 fixed-limit games. Covers starting hands, 3rd-7th street strategy for playing most hands, overcards, selective aggressiveness, reading hands, secrets of the pros, psychology, more - in a 42 "lesson" informal format. Includes bonus chapter on 7-stud tournament strategy by World Champion Tom McEvoy. 160 pages, paperback, $24.95.

**POKER TOURNAMENT TIPS FROM THE PROS** *by Shane Smith* - Essential advice from poker theorists, authors, and tournament winners on the best strategies for winning the big prizes at low-limit re-buy tournaments. Learn the best strategies for each of the four stages of play–opening, middle, late and final–how to avoid 26 potential traps, advice on re-buys, aggressive play, clock-watching, inside moves, top 20 tips for winning tournaments, more. Advice from McEvoy, Caro, Malmuth, Ciaffone, others. 102 pages, 8 1/2 x 11, spiral, $19.95.

**KEN WARREN TEACHES TEXAS HOLD 'EM** *by Ken Warren* - This is a step-by-step manual for making money at hold 'em poker. 42 powerful chapters will teach you one lesson at a time. Great practical advice and concepts accompanied by examples from actual games and how to apply them to your own games. Lessons include: Starting Cards, Playing Position, Which Hands to Play, Raising, Check-raising, Tells, Game and Seat Selection, Dominated Hands, Odds, and more. 416 pages, 6x9, paperback, $24.95.

**WINNERS GUIDE TO TEXAS HOLD 'EM POKER** *by Ken Warren* - A comprehensive book on beating hold 'em shows serious players how to play every hand from every position with every type of flop. Learn the 14 categories of starting hands, the 10 most common hold 'em tells, how to evaluate a game for profit, and more! Over 50,000 copies in print. 256 pages, 5 1/2 x 8 1/2, paperback, $14.95.

**WINNING POKER FOR THE SERIOUS PLAYER** *by Edwin Silberstang* - More than 100 actual examples provide tons of advice on beating 7 Card Stud, Texas Hold 'Em, Draw Poker, Loball, High-Low and more than 10 other variations. Silberstang analyzes the essentials of being a great player; reading tells, analyzing tables, playing position, mastering the art of deception, creating fear at the table. Also, psychological tactics, when to play aggressive or slow play, or fold, expert plays, more. Colorful glossary included. 224 pages, 5-1/2 x 8-1/2, perfect bound, $18.95.

Order Toll-Free 1-800-577-WINS or use order form on page 317

# THE CHAMPIONSHIP BOOKS
## POWERFUL BOOKS YOU MUST HAVE

**CHAMPIONSHIP OMAHA (Omaha High-Low, Pot-limit Omaha, Limit High Omaha)** *by T. J. Cloutier & Tom McEvoy.* Clearly-written strategies and powerful advice from Cloutier and McEvoy who have won four World Series of Poker titles in Omaha tournaments. Powerful advice shows you how to win at low-limit and high-stakes games, how to play against loose and tight opponents, and the differing strategies for rebuy and freezeout tournaments. Learn the best starting hands, when slowplaying a big hand is dangerous, what danglers are and why winners don't play them, why pot-limit Omaha is the only poker game where you sometimes fold the nuts on the flop and are correct in doing so and overall, how can you win a lot of money at Omaha! 230 pages, photos, illustrations, $39.95.

**CHAMPIONSHIP STUD (Seven-Card Stud, Stud 8/or Better and Razz)** *by Dr. Max Stern, Linda Johnson, and Tom McEvoy.* The authors, who have earned millions of dollars in major tournaments and cash games, eight World Series of Poker bracelets and hundreds of other titles in competition against the best players in the world show you the winning strategies for medium-limit side games as well as poker tournaments and a general tournament strategy that is applicable to any form of poker. Includes give-and-take conversations between the authors to give you more than one point of view on how to play poker. 200 pages, hand pictorials, photos. $29.95.

**CHAMPIONSHIP HOLD'EM** *by T. J. Cloutier & Tom McEvoy.* Hard-hitting hold'em the way it's played *today* in both limit cash games and tournaments. Get killer advice on how to win more money in rammin'-jammin' games, kill-pot, jackpot, shorthanded, and other types of cash games. You'll learn the thinking process before the flop, on the flop, on the turn, and at the river with specific suggestions for what to do when good or bad things happen plus 20 illustrated hands with play-by-play analyses. Specific advice for rocks in tight games, weaklings in loose games, experts in solid games, how hand values change in jackpot games, when you should fold, check, raise, reraise, check-raise, slowplay, bluff, and tournament strategies for small buy-in, big buy-in, rebuy, incremental add-on, satellite and big-field major tournaments. Wow! Easy-to-read and conversational, if you want to become a lifelong winner at limit hold'em, you need this book! 320 Pages, Illustrated, Photos. $39.95

**CHAMPIONSHIP NO-LIMIT & POT LIMIT HOLD'EM** *by T. J. Cloutier & Tom McEvoy* The definitive guide to winning at two of the world's most exciting poker games! Written by eight time World Champion players T. J. Cloutier (1998 Player of the Year) and Tom McEvoy (the foremost author on tournament strategy) who have won millions of dollars playing no-limit and pot-limit hold'em in cash games and major tournaments around the world. You'll get all the answers here - no holds barred - to your most important questions: How do you get inside your opponents' heads and learn how to beat them at their own game? How can you tell how much to bet, raise, and reraise in no-limit hold'em? When can you bluff? How do you set up your opponents in pot-limit hold'em so that you can win a monster pot? What are the best strategies for winning no-limit and pot-limit tournaments, satellites, and supersatellites? You get rock-solid and inspired advice from two of the most recognizable figures in poker — advice that you can bank on. If you want to become a winning player, a champion, you must have this book. 209 pages, paperback, illustrations, photos. $39.95

**Order Toll-Free 1-800-577-WINS or use order form on page 317**

# OTHER BOOKS BY MIKE CARO
## THE MAD GENIUS OF POKER

**CARO'S GUIDE TO DOYLE BRUNSON'S SUPER SYSTEM** - Working with World Champion Doyle Brunson, the legendary Mike Caro has created a fresh look to the "Bible" of all poker books, adding new and personal insights that help you understand the original work. Caro breaks 36 concepts into either "Analysis, Commentary, Concept, Mission, Play-By-Play, Psychology, Statistics, Story, or Strategy. Lots of illustrations and winning concepts give even more value to this great work. 86 pages, 8 1/2 x 11, stapled. $19.95.

**CARO'S FUNDAMENTAL SECRETS OF WINNING POKER** - The world's foremost poker theoretician and strategist presents the essential strategies, concepts, and secret winning plays that comprise the very foundation of winning poker play. Shows how to win more from weak players, equalize stronger players, bluff a bluffer, win big pots, where to sit against weak players, the six factors of strategic table image. Includes selected tips on hold 'em, 7 stud, draw, lowball, tournaments, more. 160 Pages, 5 1/2 x 8 1/2, perfect bound, $12.95.

**Call Toll Free (800)577-WINS or Use Coupon Below to Order Books, Videos & Software**

## BECOME A BETTER POKER PLAYER!

**YES!** I want to be a winner! Rush me the following items: (Write in choices below):

| Quantity | Your Book Order | Price |
|---|---|---|
|  |  |  |
|  |  |  |
|  |  |  |
|  |  |  |
|  |  |  |
|  |  |  |

**MAKE CHECKS TO:**
Cardoza Publishing
P.O. Box 1500, Cooper Station
New York, NY 10276
**CHARGE BY PHONE:**
Toll-Free:    1-800-577-WINS
E-Mail Orders: CardozaPub@aol.com

| | |
|---|---|
| Subtotal | |
| Postage/Handling: First Item | $5 00 |
| Additional Postage | |
| Total Amount Due | |

SHIPPING CHARGES: For US orders, include $5.00 postage/handling 1st book ordered; for each additional book, add $1.00. For Canada/Mexico, double above amounts, quadruple (4X) for all other countries. Orders outside U.S., money order payable in U.S. dollars on U.S. bank only.

NAME _____

ADDRESS _____

CITY _____ STATE _____ ZIP _____

**30 day money back guarantee!**                    Caro Tells 2003

# VIDEOS BY MIKE CARO
## THE MAD GENIUS OF POKER

### CARO'S PRO POKER TELLS

The long-awaited two-video set is a powerful scientific course on how to use your opponents' gestures, words and body language to read their hands and win all their money. These carefully guarded poker secrets, filmed with 63 poker notables, will revolutionize your game. It reveals when opponents are bluffing, when they aren't, and why. Knowing what your opponent's gestures mean, and protecting them from knowing yours, gives you a huge winning edge. *An absolute must buy!* $59.95.

### CARO'S MAJOR POKER SEMINAR

The legendary "Mad Genius" is at it again, giving poker advice in VHS format. This new tape is based on the inaugural class at Mike Caro University of Poker, Gaming and Life strategy. The material given on this tape is based on many fundamentals introduced in Caro's books, papers, and articles and is prepared in such a way that reinforces concepts old and new. Caro's style is easy-going but intense with key concepts stressed and re-peated. This tape will improve your play. 60 Minutes. $24.95.

### CARO'S POWER POKER SEMINAR

This powerful video shows you how to win big money using the little-known concepts of world champion players. This advice will be worth thousands of dollars to you every year, even more if you're a big money player! After 15 years of refusing to allow his seminars to be filmed, Caro presents entertaining but serious coverage of his long-guarded secrets. Contains the most profitable poker advice ever put on video. 62 Minutes! $39.95.

Order Toll-Free 1-800-577-WINS or use order form on page 317

# POWERFUL POKER SIMULATIONS
**A** MUST FOR SERIOUS PLAYERS WITH A COMPUTER!
IBM compatibles CD ROM Windows 3.1, 95, and 98 - Full Color Graphics

**Play interactive poker** against these **incredible** full color poker simulation programs - they're the absolute **best** method to improve game. *Computer players act like real players.* All games let you set the limits and rake, have fully programmable players, adjustable lineup, stat tracking, and Hand Analyzer for starting hands. MIke Caro, the world's foremost poker theoretician says, *"Amazing...A steal for under $500...get it, it's great."* Includes *free telephone support.* **New Feature!** - "Smart advisor" gives expert advice for *every* play in *every* game!

**I. TURBO TEXAS HOLD'EM FOR WINDOWS - $89.95** - Choose which players, how many, 2-10, you want to play, create loose/tight game, control check-raising, bluffing, position, sensitivity to pot odds, more! Also, instant replay, pop-up odds, Professional Advisor, keeps track of play statistics. Free bonus: *Hold'em Hand Analyzer* analyzes all 169 pocket hands in detail, their win rates under any conditions you set. Caro says this *"hold'em software is the most powerful ever created."* Great product!

**2. TURBO SEVEN-CARD STUD FOR WINDOWS - $89.95** - *Create any conditions of play*, choose number of players (2-8), bet amounts, fixed or spread limit, bring-in method, tight/loose conditions, position, reaction to board, number of dead cards, stack deck to create special conditions, instant replay. Terrific stat reporting includes analysis of starting cards, 3-D bar charts, graphs. Play interactively, run high speed simulation to test strategies. *Hand Analyzer* analyzes starting hands in detail. Wow!

**3. TURBO OMAHA HIGH-LOW SPLIT FOR WINDOWS - $89.95** -Specify any playing conditions; betting limits, number of raises, blind structures, button position, aggressiveness/passiveness of opponents, number of players (2-10), types of hands dealt, blinds, position, board reaction, specify flop, turn, river cards! Choose opponents, use provided point count or create your own. Statistical reporting, instant replay, pop-up odds, high speed simulation to test strategies, amazing Hand Analyzer, much more!

**4. TURBO OMAHA HIGH FOR WINDOWS - $89.95** - Same features as above, but tailored for the Omaha High-only game. Caro says program is *"an electrifying research tool...it can clearly be worth thousands of dollars to any serious player.* A must for Omaha High players.

**5. TURBO 7 STUD 8 OR BETTER - $89.95** - Brand new with all the features you expect from the Wilson Turbo products: the latest artificial intelligence, instant advice and exact odds, play versus 2-7 opponents, enhanced data charts that can be exported or printed, the ability to fold out of turn and immediately go to the next hand, ability to peek at opponents hand, optional warning mode that warns you if a play disagrees with the advisor, and automatic testing mode that can run up to 50 tests unattended. Challenge tough computer players who vary their styles for a truly great poker game.

**6. TOURNAMENT TEXAS HOLD'EM - $59.95**

Set-up for tournament practice and play, this realistic simulation pits you against celebrity look-alikes. Tons of options let you control tournament size with 10 to 300 entrants, select limits, ante, rake, blind structures, freezeouts, number of rebuys and competition level of opponents - average, tough, or toughest. Pop-up status report shows how you're doing vs. the competition. Save tournaments in progress to play again later. Additional feature allows you to quickly finish a folded hand and go on to the next.

**Order Toll-Free 1-800-577-WINS or use order form on page 317**